SECRET ST ALBANS

Kate Morris

AMBERLEY

Acknowledgements

I should like to thank so many friends, relatives and colleagues who have helped to make this book what it is – the story and picture of life in St Albans in the long eighteenth century. In particular I must mention Pat Howe, Professor Sarah Lloyd, and Roger Miles, colleagues at the St Albans Museum Service, SAHAAS and the Harpenden LHS, but many more have given their support in various ways and I hope that they will all enjoy the end result. I have made every effort to attribute the illustrations I have used correctly and appreciate the many sources I have used.

Abbreviations

HALS – Hertfordshire Archives and Local Studies
SAHAAS – St Albans & Hertfordshire Architectural & Archaeological Society
TNA – The National Archives
SAMS – St Albans Museum Service
Harpenden LHS – Harpenden Local History Society

First published 2020

Amberley Publishing
The Hill, Stroud
Gloucestershire, GL5 4EP

www.amberley-books.com

ISBN 978 1 4456 9073 5 (print)
ISBN 978 1 4456 9074 2 (ebook)

British Library Cataloguing in Publication Data.
A catalogue record for this book is available from the British Library.

Typesetting by SJmagic DESIGN SERVICES, India.
Printed in Great Britain.

Contents

Introduction

St Albans, a city by royal edict of 1877, offers much to delight and surprise its interested community: Roman Verulamium, the Abbey Church and Great Gateway, the only surviving medieval belfry in this country and a charter of 1553 granting borough status, though this latter status was lost under the Local Government Act 1972.

This book provides insights into the social history of the charter borough with examples from the period between the Glorious Revolution of 1688 and the reform era of the 1830s. Lying just 20 miles from London on the major highway to the industrial Midlands, the North West and on to Ireland, it was, as described in Asa Briggs' chapter celebrating the city's centenary, even at its most parochial, never provincial, its thoroughfare location ensuring significance in all periods of English history.[1] The continuing importance of the route, which passed through the town's Market Place, always busy with traders, wagons, coaches, and individual travellers, was guaranteed by Telford's turnpike improvements, until, in the 1830s, the town was bypassed by the nation's new railway network. Market and fair days saw stalls and entertainments of all kinds. Inns and taverns provided accommodation for passing traffic and venues for locals. Proximity to London meant access to luxury goods and easy contact for business and social interactions not so readily available to market towns further afield. The town's good water, clean air and fresh produce from the surrounding farms made it a good place in which to live. Not surprising then that the gentry were attracted to the town, providing employment for servants, and trade for its shops. Farmworkers also lived in the town.

The borough's charter provided for a mayor, elected annually from amongst the twelve principal burgesses, who was responsible for law and order and control of the Wednesday and Saturday markets. Principal burgesses, or aldermen, were elected by their peers, always within a week of the death or removal of one of their number, and held office for life – a classic case of waiting for dead men's shoes.

The population of St Albans was little more than 3,000 in the seventeenth century and, by 1801, still only 3,872. This growth however continued into the nineteenth century, to 6,582 in 1831. Boundary extensions reflected the increase, which sped up once the railways finally connected the town directly with London and the North in the 1860s.

As well as employment for men, the town provided an option for women with straw plaiting as supplementary home work, so the town never saw real poverty. At election times income, as well as entertainment, was provided by the treating of voters. Until the passing of the Reform Act in 1832, this extended here to all ratepayers as well as property owners and freemen. Markets and fairs, antiquarian finds and historic institutions and hostelries all contributed to the town's tourism offer, which also stimulated the economy.

St Albans represents the history of the country as a whole over time, but local eighteenth-century stories can still surprise, since, as Briggs continues, 'we know less of this town than we do of other larger conurbations, despite its being a "town with a past" as transport hub, political pawn and attractive tourist destination'. It is this heritage which continues to attract incoming residents and visitors alike.

1. The Town's Layout and Built Environment

The boundaries of the town, planned on this strategic route from the City of London by one of St Albans' medieval abbots on the hill above his monastery, were well defined and are still identifiable today. Regular 'beating of the bounds' reminded inhabitants in case of doubt. This was a perambulation of the town's 4-mile perimeter from Black Cross on Fishpool Street, across to the Stone Cross at the northern boundary and then down what is now Marlborough Road, by the Tonman Ditch to the river at Sopwell. The river formed the boundary back along to St Michael's.

The town's position generated enormous traffic and business for its market. However, in 1665 it was said, 'The miles between Hell and any other place on earth, were shorter than those between London and St Albans.' The introduction of the turnpike system

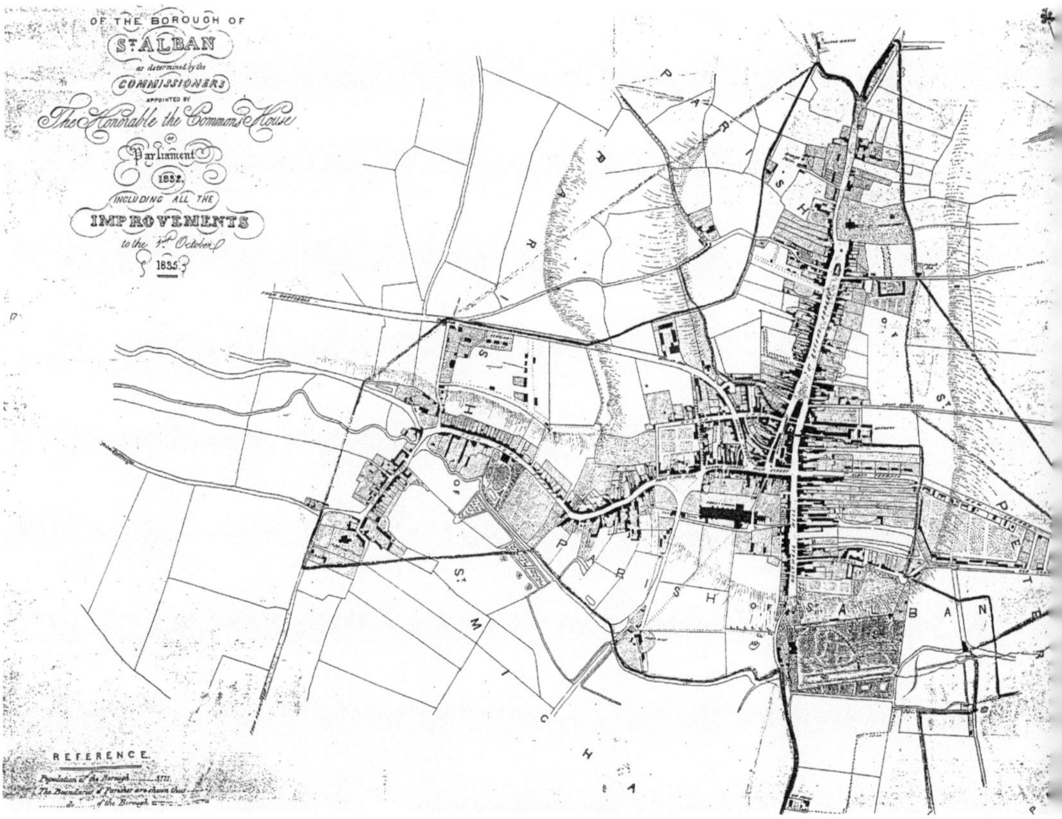

The borough was extended in 1832 to reflect a population then of 5,571. (SAMS)

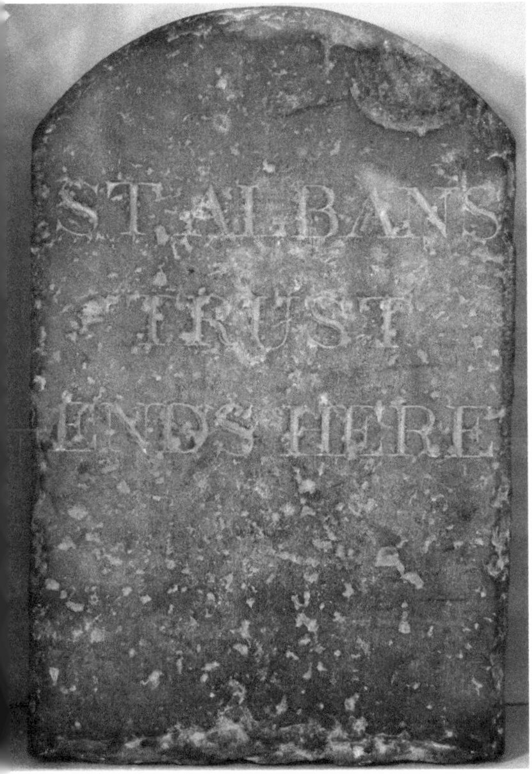

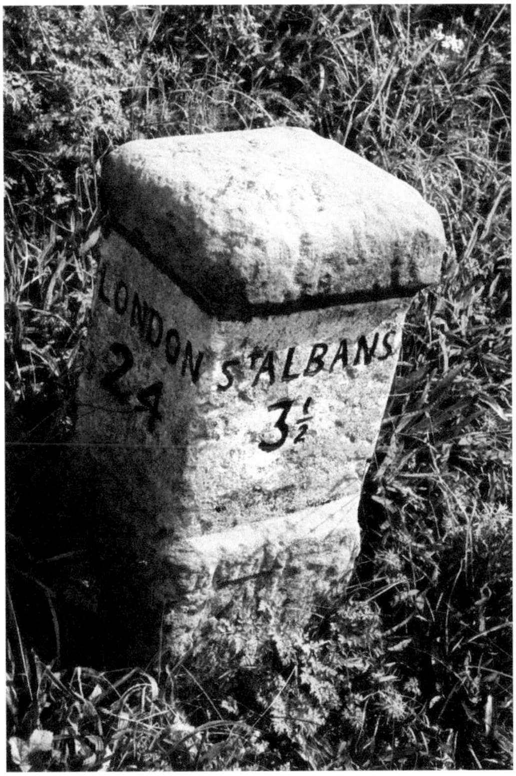

Above left: The stone marked the limit of the Trust's responsibility. (SAMS)

Above right: Milestone 3 ½ miles along the Dunstable turnpike. (Darnell collection © SAHAAS)

brought much-needed improvements to the roads and the erection of signposts. St Albans Turnpike Trust, established in 1715, was responsible for the road from South Mimms to Bow Bridge on the Redbourn Road and another trust continued the route to Dunstable.

The St Albans turnpike entered the town along Sopwell Lane, continued up the hill, turning left at the Peahen corner to the Market Cross on High Street, and then down Fishpool Street and up what is now the drive to Gorhambury, reaching the Redbourn Road just beyond the present-day Prae Wood Arms restaurant. This route was crossed in the town by the Hatfield to Reading turnpike, which formed a London by-pass for travellers from the north and east en route for that favourite eighteenth-century watering place, Bath. These routes can still be recognised in the layout of the town's centre, attractive, but, as ever, frequently causing gridlock. Telford's cutting of both London Road and Verulam Road, thus by-passing both Holywell Hill and Fishpool Street, will have improved the situation then, but only contributes to the traffic problems of today!

The medieval belfry in the Market Place we know as the Clock Tower, built by the townspeople in the early fifteenth century as a sort of town hall, provided a shop at ground-floor level, with accommodation above reached by a separate stairway. The great bell Gabriel traditionally sounded the Angelus and the curfew. During the

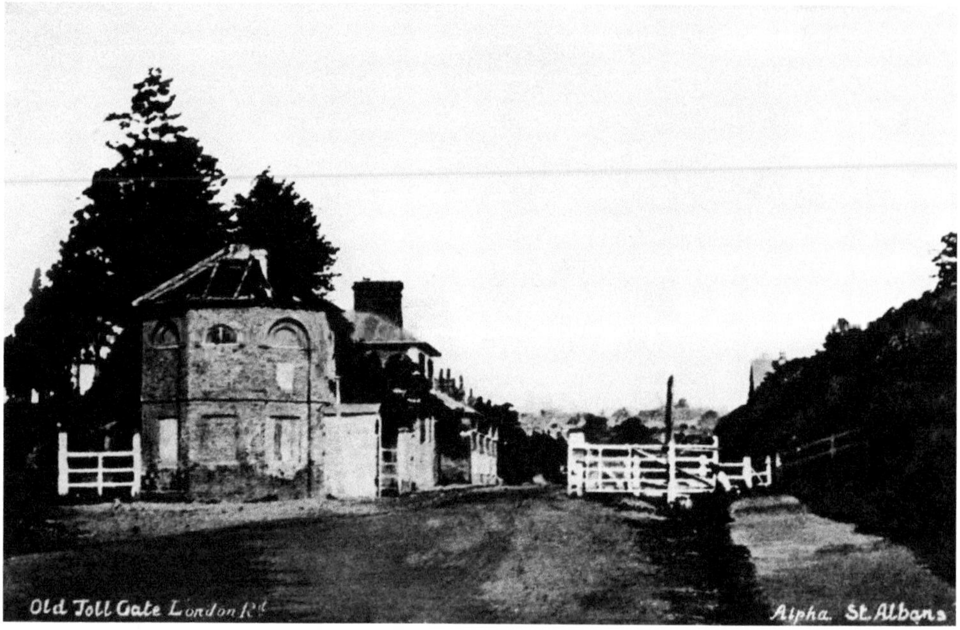

Tollgate on the new London Road cut, in 1795, by Thomas Telford. (Copyright reserved) (SAMS)

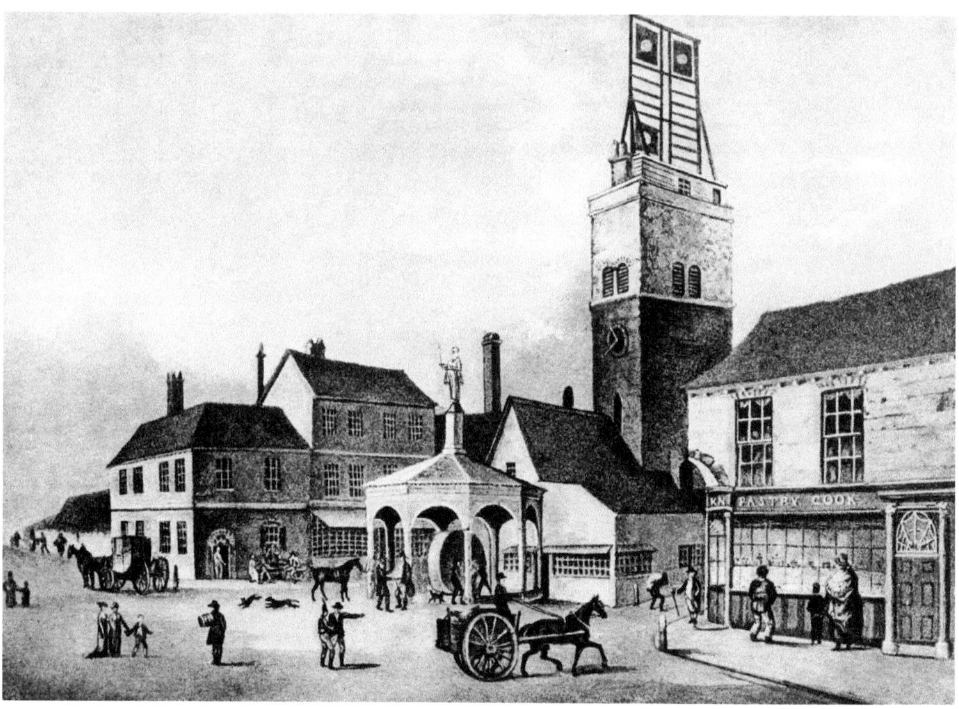

Market Cross and Clock Tower with semaphore signalling station. Reproduction of an aquatint by Sutherland *c.* 1812. (SAMS)

Napoleonic Wars, the tower was one of the signalling stations connecting London with Yarmouth for Admiralty communications which took only between five and seventeen minutes if the operators were on the ball and weather permitted. The view from the top on a clear day extends almost to London.

The eighteenth century saw building booms across the country, and St Albans provided no exception. Popular among gentry folk with frequent need to be in London, many built or bought houses here, often retaining lodgings or chambers in the capital. Merchants would divide their time between their London business houses and their family homes 'in the country'.

New houses were typically in the classical style seen on the Grand Tour and were built of brick. This provided greater security from fire risk and also commanded lower premiums with the burgeoning insurance companies than the traditional timber-framed and thatched houses.

There is little building stone in the area, apart from soft Totternhoe clunch and over-hard flint but the clay earth in Hertfordshire is good for brick-making and this art, lost in this country with the withdrawal of the Romans in the fifth century, again became a lucrative industry. In the intervening centuries bricks from the ruins of Verulamium had however frequently been recycled for high-status structures, like the abbey.

Flint, although of little use for construction, forms a large part of a geological feature unique to Hertfordshire, which was often incorporated in buildings as a token considered to bring good fortune. Puddingstone is a particularly hard conglomerate of flint pebbles cemented by silica.

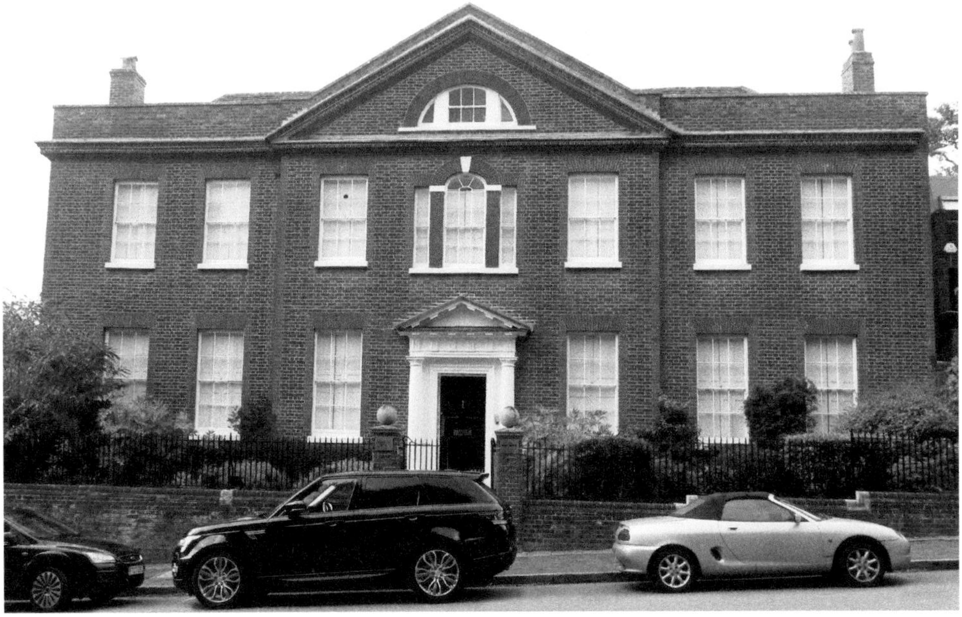

Romeland House, built *c.* 1762 for London merchant Frederick Vandermeulen. (Kari Lundgaard)

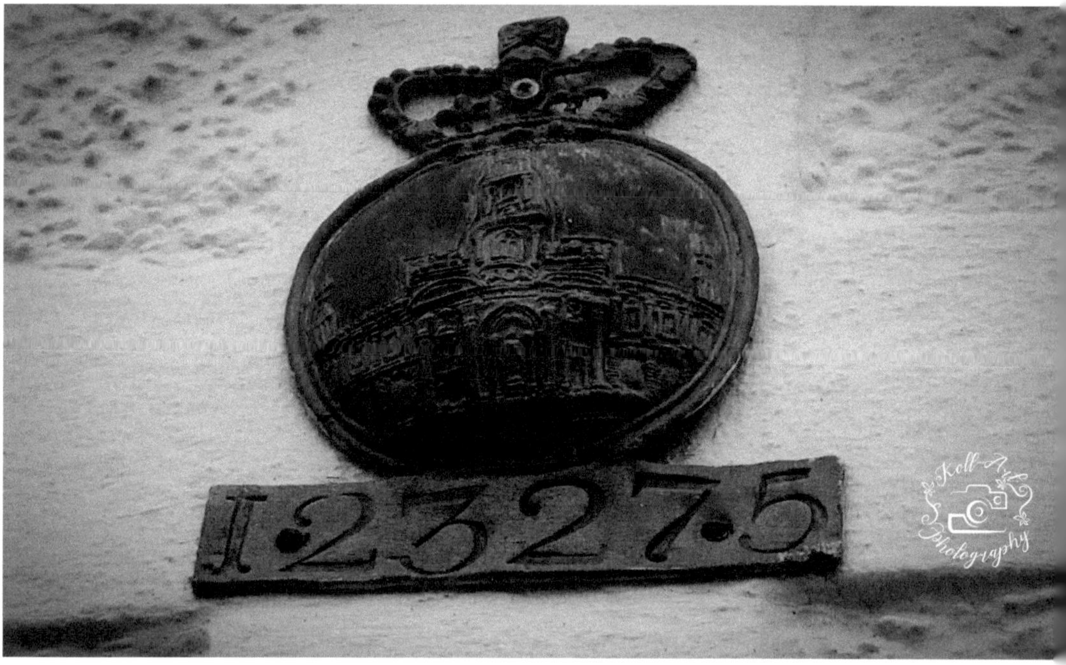

Royal Exchange Insurance fire-mark on a house on Holywell Hill. (Koll-Art Photography)

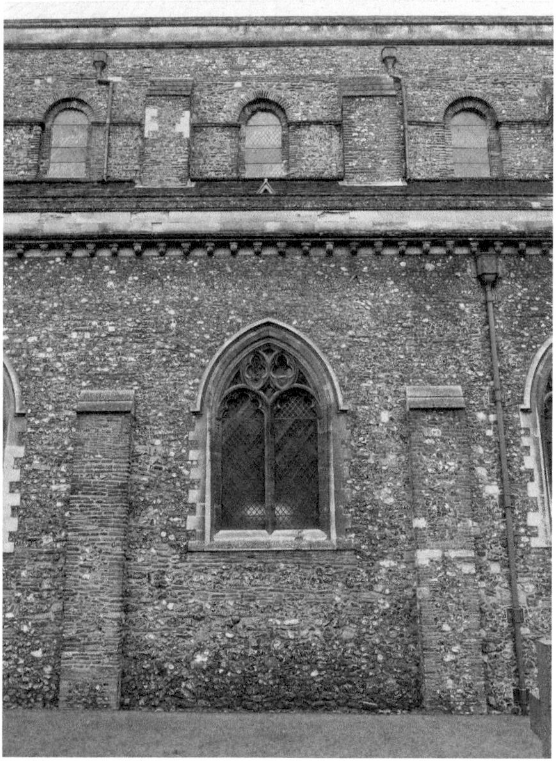

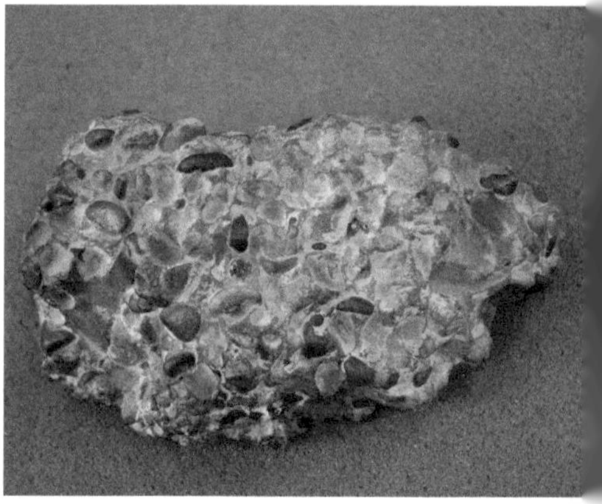

Above: An example of Hertfordshire puddingstone. (Frank Iddiols)

Left: Roman bricks used by the Norman abbots for the Abbey Church. (Kari Lundgaard)

One of the most beautiful examples of local brickwork can be found in the church of St Saviours on Sandpit Lane, built in the early twentieth century to serve the Bernards Heath brick-making community. Brick-making ceased in the area in the 1940s but the handmade bricks used for the cathedral's new Welcome Centre continue the tradition.

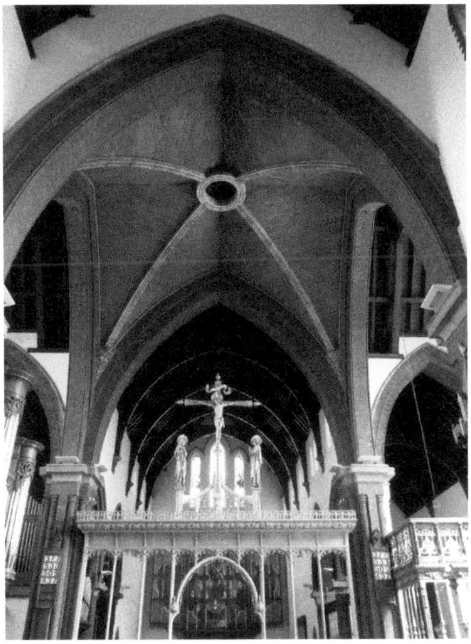

Right: Locally made bricks feature in the beautifully crafted interior of St Saviour's Church. (Kari Lundgaard)

Below: The cathedral and Abbey Church's new Welcome Centre featuring handmade, though not local, bricks. (Kari Lundgaard)

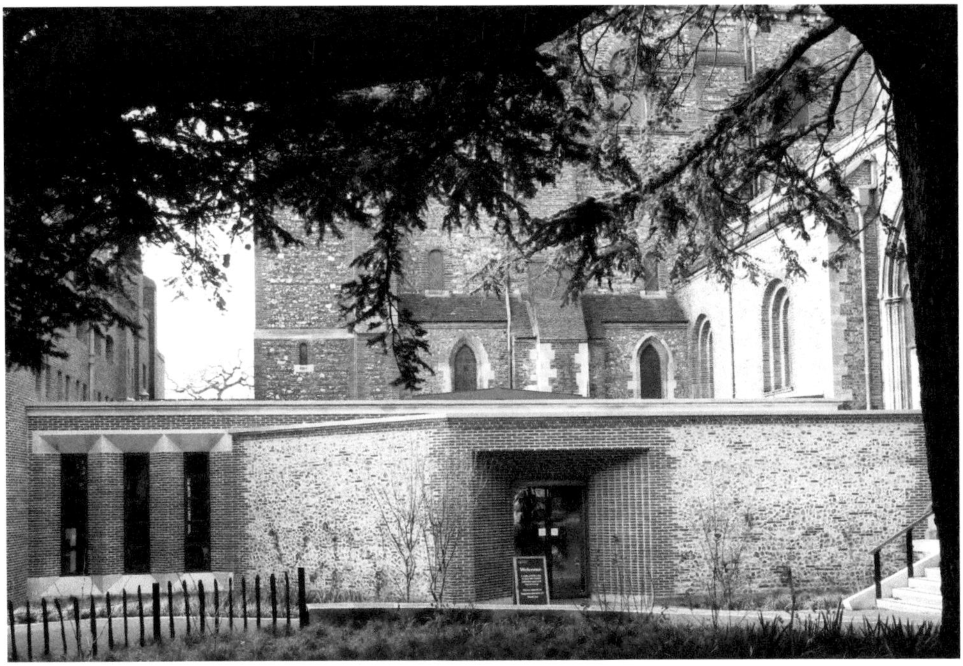

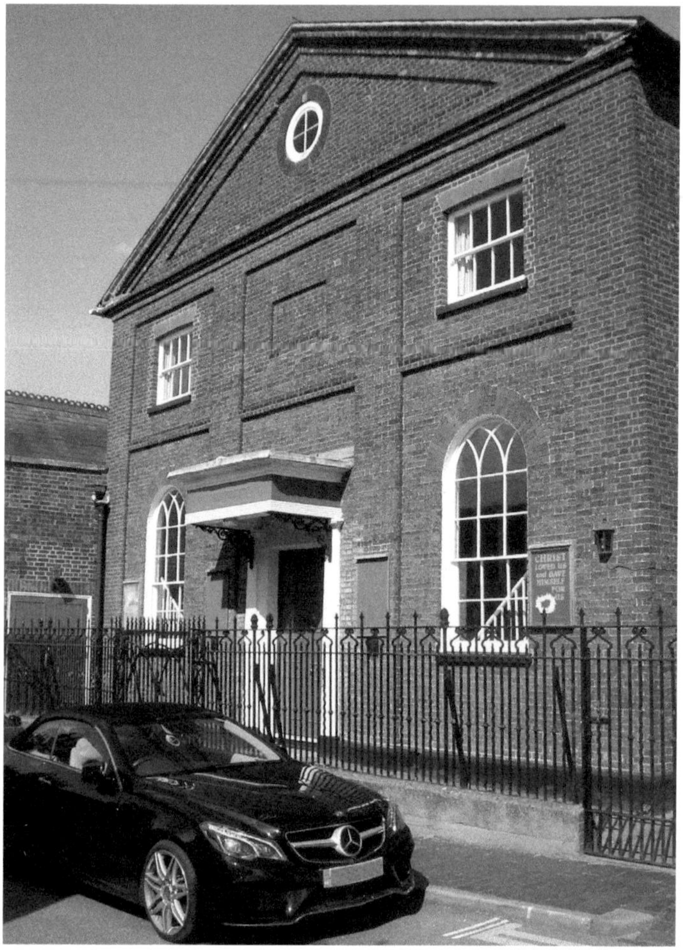

Spicer Street Independent Church, built 1812. (David Smart)

Substantial communities of Independents, Presbyterians, Baptists, Methodists and Quakers grew up in the town, most of which are still active today. From the late seventeenth century onwards, their chapels appeared on vacant land around Dagnall Lane, behind the market and the main highway.

DID YOU KNOW?

St Albans Clock Tower was one of the eighteen stations on the shutter telegraph signalling system which could convey news from the Admiralty in London to Yarmouth during the Napoleonic Wars in seventeen minutes, subject only to adverse weather conditions, such as fog. This extension of the systems along the south coast was completed in 1808 but dismantled at the end of the war in 1815.

2. The Town – A Transport Hub

DID YOU KNOW?

Although in the seventeenth century it was still usual for it to take a day to travel from St Albans to London, by the early nineteenth century it was possible to travel there and back to conduct business all in a day, though not as fast as by train today. In 1735, on a horse, the journey could be made in little more than an hour, though coaches took a little longer.

By the eighteenth century, wagons were replacing the packhorse trains, which had brought goods from as far as Kendal to the capital. Wagons carried more goods and required fewer horses. An advertisement of 1836 for 'The Original Wagon Service' based in High Street boasts of having been established here in 1721. Wagons also carried passengers, though an increasing number of coaches also plied the routes. Coach services to London from

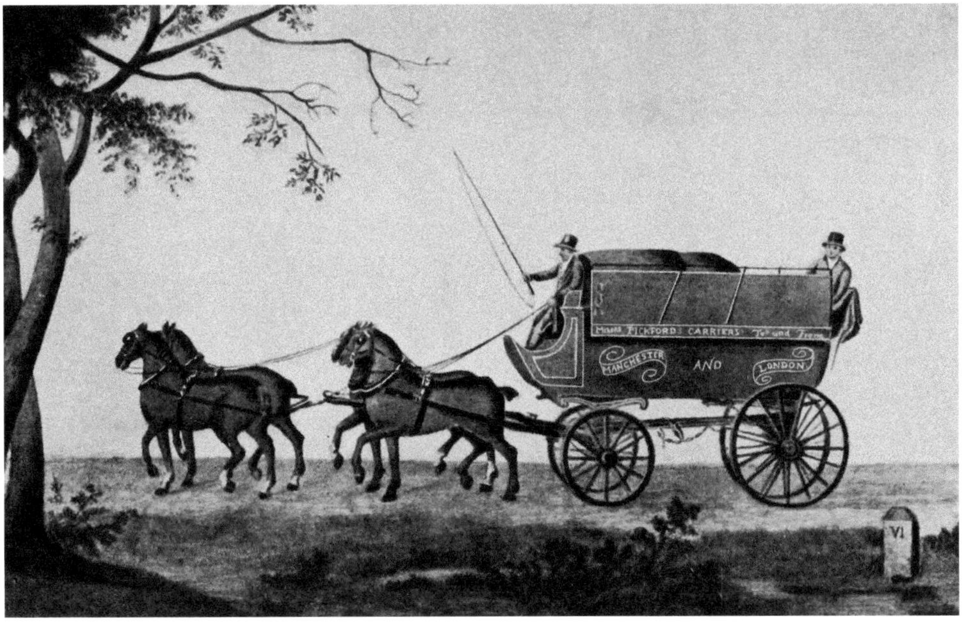

Pickford's London and Manchester Fly wagon, which was light and required only four horses.

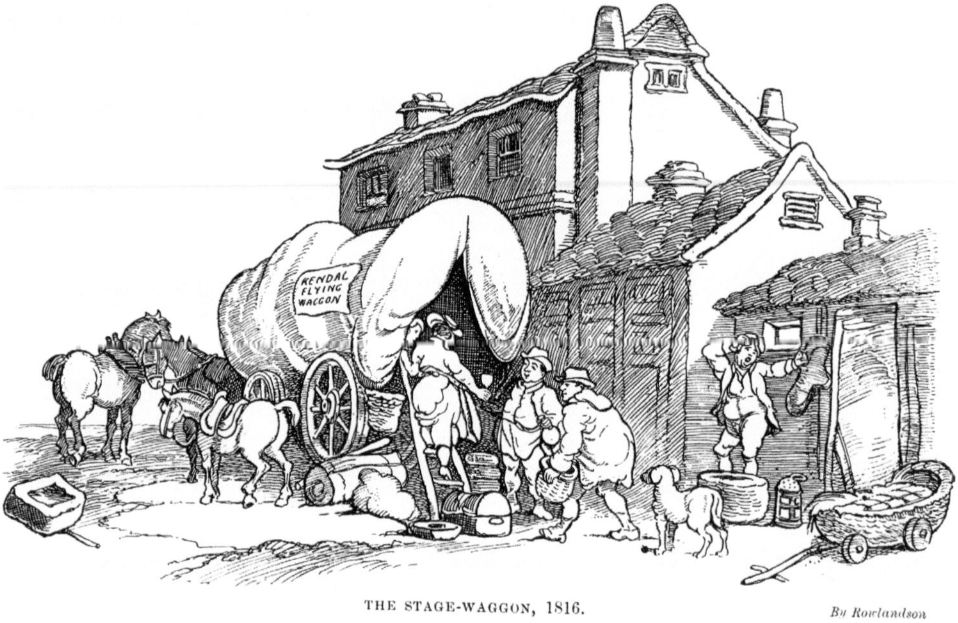

Passengers joining the stage wagon in Kendal, drawn by Thomas Rowlandson, 1816.

St Albans included one from the George Inn to The Ram in Smithfield, and another from the Flower de Luce in Market Place to the Cock in Aldersgate. This one ran on alternate days, returning always the following day.

Lying on the principal route from the North West, St Albans' inns provided stabling and accommodation for the long-distance carriers, though the establishment of out-of-town depots, such as that Thomas Pickford set up in 1768 at Markyate, reduced that demand. Passing traffic was, however, still huge and it was said by the early nineteenth century, some seventy coaches a day entered the town. Speed was not generally a priority, but competition between coachmen did lead to frequent bets over best times and a wager in 1744 saw a coach arrive in St Albans from an inn in Piccadilly in two hours five minutes.

Comfort was a different matter as we see from a letter written by the twenty-three-year-old son of Alderman Jasper Arris Borradale of Hall Place. Young George, of whom also more later, wrote, in 1755, to his Colonel, describing his journey from London on the 'St Albans Machine'. After enduring the company of three children, a baby and a dog, as well as three persons sick and one woman drunk on mulled wine on this 'caravan' for 10 miles, he abandoned the coach and hired a post-chaise to complete the trip.[2]

The end of the nineteenth century saw steam coaches passing through the town, carrying more passengers, though this development was short-lived – it was thought that these larger vehicles would damage the roads and frighten the horses. In fact, their demise was largely due to the high tolls they were charged and then the laying of railways which allowed even more passengers to be carried.

Troops used this route when marching against the Scots and travelling to Ireland. Following the victory over the Jacobites in 1745, returning troops brought Lord Lovat for

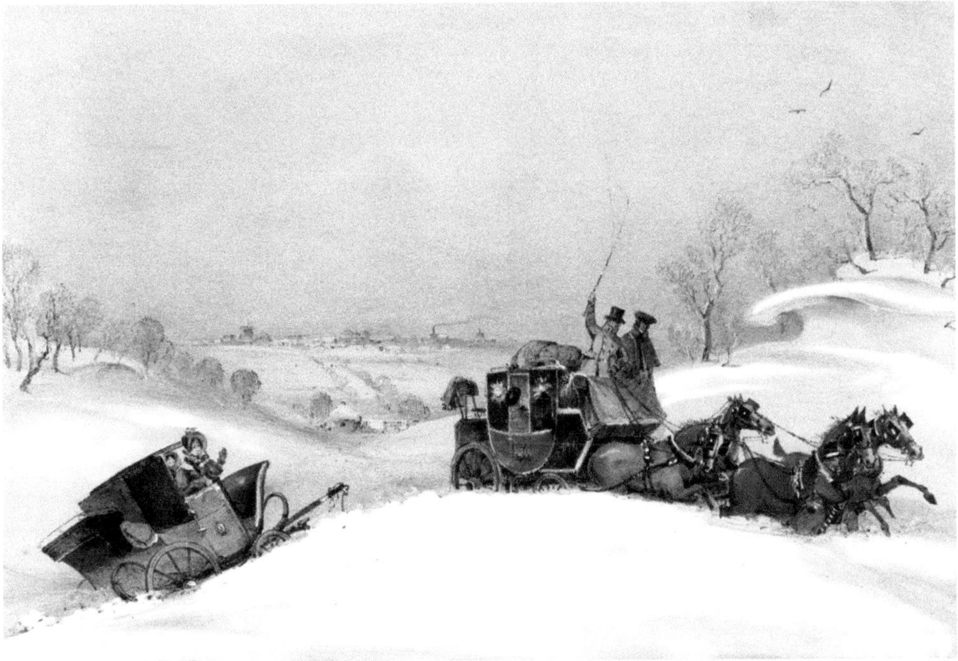

The Liverpool coach and a chariot caught in the snowstorm of December 1836 just south of St Albans, by James Pollard. (SAMS)

trial in London, stopping over at the White Hart Inn on Holywell Hill. This inn survives today, despite comment in 1792 by the diarist John Byng that it was 'perhaps the best here', but 'unequalled in filth, inattention and charge'. Whilst there, Lovat's portrait was painted by William Hogarth, in the town at the invitation of his friend Dr Joshua Webster. Webster has been said to be the son of the Old Pretender. Whilst living in St Albans, he was active as an antiquarian and also invented his Cerevisia Anglicana, or the English Herb Diet-Drink, which continued to sell well into the nineteenth century.

By horse the journey to the capital was faster. For a forty-guinea wager, two men rode to the turnpike at Battle Bridge (Kings Cross) in 1735 in one hour six minutes, though one horse arrived with a badly injured foot and the other died the following day. Many also travelled on foot, equally often for wagers. In 1727 a boy ran from Essex Street in London to St Albans and back in seven hours, faster than the estimate.

Whilst a journey to the capital for Sir Nicholas Bacon had taken a day from Gorhambury, when Lord Keeper of the Great Seal to Good Queen Bess, by 1814, Sir William Domville, Lord Mayor of London, could visit London, conduct his business in the City and still return to his house on Holywell Hill in his own post-chaise in a day.

Local travel was a different matter. Much was on foot or by cart, or chaise, but those whose means were sufficient might have been carried by two chairmen. In 1762, Ann, a daughter of Joshua Lomax MP, of Childwickbury, and the wife of Thomas Beech, a wealthy brewer of Redbourn, in her will left her sedan chair to her friend Ruth, wife of tinman Jacob Warner.

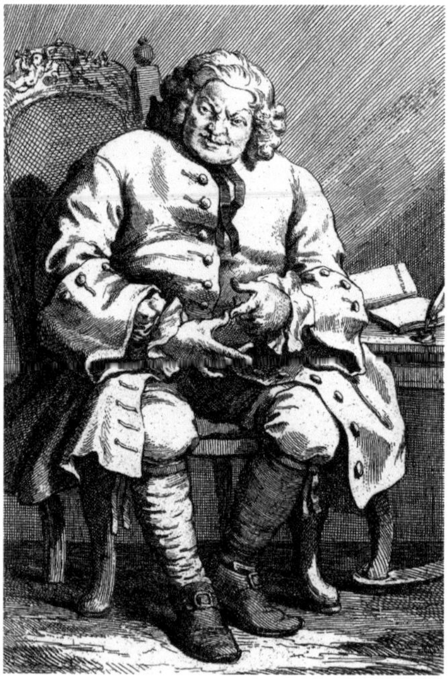

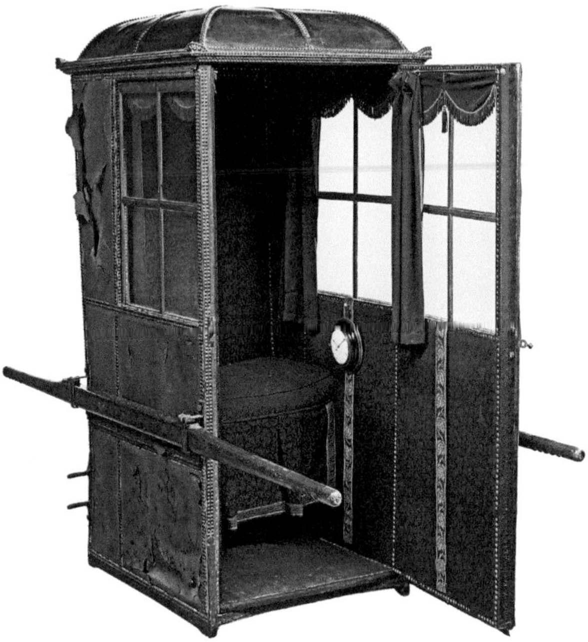

Above left: Simon, Lord Lovat, at the White Hart in 1745, by William Hogarth. (SAMS)

Above right: Sedan chair, possibly similar to that of Ann Beech, sold at Christie's in 2013. (© 2013 Christie's Images Ltd)

A local farmer drove into the town in 1835 in a cart pulled by four large hogs. They arrived at a brisk trot and caused such a sensation he was offered fifty pounds for this unusual mode of transport, but refused to sell. He had apparently been training the pigs for around six months.

Transport and travel arrangements for business reasons, or perhaps to enjoy 'the season', required much organisation. The Grimstons' accounts reveal much in the way of packing and unpacking and caretaking as they split their time between Gorhambury and their house in Grosvenor Square.

Revd Robert Rumney, vicar of St Peter's, St Albans, from 1715 to 1743, had a mansion opposite the church,[3] but, in 1720, appointed his brother curate and took up lodgings in London, having secured the post of lecturer at St Giles without Cripplegate, a parish now developed as the Barbican estate. The family also had a country estate, Bemonds, so there will have been much travelling to accommodate family and professional life, as well as entertaining in the town itself.

3. The Chilterns Chalk and the Town's River and Water Supply

St Albans lies by the River Ver on Chiltern chalk. Rainwater is stored in this chalk and finds its way through fissures in the rock to feed the river and, until the mid-nineteenth century when clean water could be piped to individual houses and standpipes in the town, supplied the many wells. Industries have valued the river's water power and the townspeople its pure well water, lauded by Dr Joshua Webster for 'being philtered through a stratum of chalk', and no doubt the basis of his Cerevisia Anglicana.[4] Chalk streams such as the Ver are unusual features found only in a few parts of the world.

The seven mills along the banks of the river from Shafford to Park Street ground corn and produced paper, and, later, silk and cotton. Seventeenth-century tanners used the river water, and glover John Ruth rented ground by Bing's Orchard, at Sopwell, for washing and scouring his hides and skins. Householders and inns in the town had their own wells and for animals there were ponds and cisterns on St Peter's Street, fed from springs on higher ground to the north. These ponds also supported the town's fire engines.

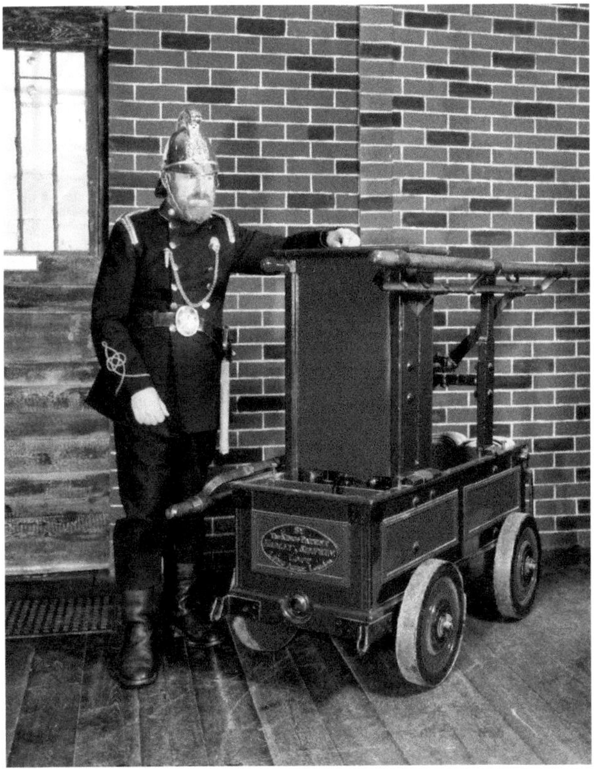

Victorian fire engine in the collection of the St Albans Museum Service. (SAMS)

DID YOU KNOW?

Boundary Road, only made up in 1912, marks the extension of the borough boundaries to include what was then known as Sandridge New Town, the home of the Bernards Heath brick-making community.

The geology of Bernards Heath provided a layer of clay for brick-makers. Below, the water-bearing chalk could also usefully be mined. Deep ponds were created from these activities which provided a source of water but danger for both people and animals. Nineteen-year- old agricultural labourer Henry Spriggs drowned there in 1871 and on another occasion a horse was lost in the same way. The seasonal nature of brick-making meant it was often combined with other trades, such as well-sinking. The Fowler family worked at both, as did several generations of the Butcher family. The Butchers' story has been written in some detail in a typescript deposited in the SAHAAS library. Charles Butcher settled in Adelaide Street around 1840, working as a flint cutter and well-sinker. Four of his sons took to the same trades and lived close to their work on Bernards Heath. The rough settlement there, known at first as Sandridge New Town, only became part of the borough in 1879 and the roads were not made up until 1912. Sons Joe and Charles Butcher continued to practise their trade from Culver Road for the rest of their lives, as did some of the following generation.

At some points on the Heath, the water table could be reached through the clay quite easily, but the inns, where a supply of water had to be guaranteed, sometimes dug very

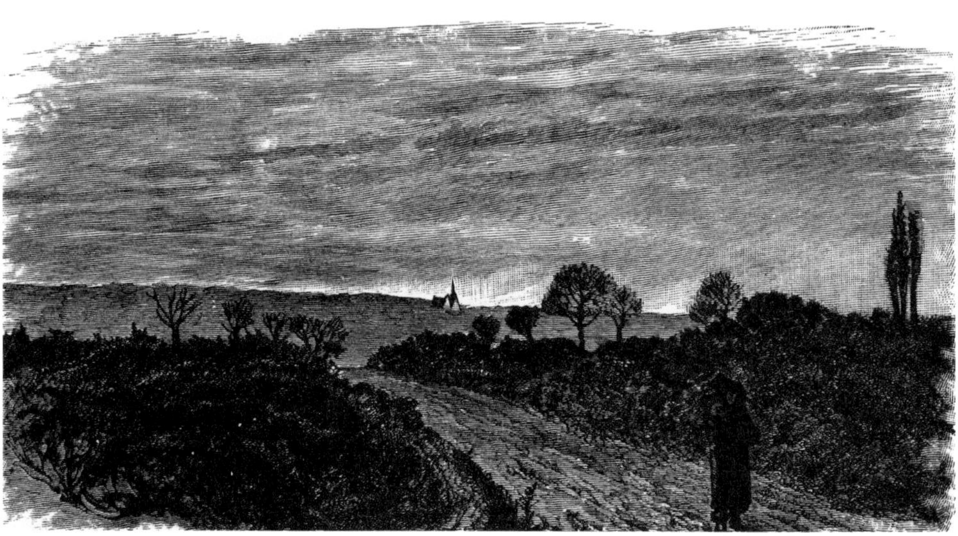

Bernard's Heath was unfriendly, though rich in clay for bricks and chalk for both mining and water supply. (SAMS)

deep wells. Thomas Baskerville, staying at the Red Lion, close to the Clock Tower, in 1682, commented that the well there was some 40 fathoms deep, or nearly 75 metres, a source of pride, no doubt, to his landlady, Mrs Selioke.

Sinking wells is both dangerous and expensive, with many recorded accidents. A 1735 newspaper report tells of a fall of earth on a man at the bottom of a deep well, leaving only his head and one arm free. A companion went down and managed to free the other arm, fixing a rope under the man's armpits, but he could not be freed. Despite the surrounding earth being dug out all weekend, more loose earth dropped into the well, helpers had to be pulled up and the poor man was finally smothered.

The source of power to draw the water from these wells was sometimes just a man or animal, but pumps have also been in use for at least 2,000 years. Piston pumps distributed water to London subscribers throughout the seventeenth century, whilst from the time of Sir Samuel Morland's patent of 1674, the plunger pump was also in use. Many towns previously without good water were provided with piped water supply from nearby rivers in the period following. Plumbers John and William Yarnold were in demand for such installations all over the country.

Around St Albans, animal power was still used on country estates – either a donkey wheel or a horse mill with a rope wound round a capstan to draw up the buckets. A donkey wheel at St Julian's, on Watling Street, reached the national press on 21 August 1725 when the following report appeared in the Ipswich Journal:

> an Ass that had gone into the Wheel to draw Water 14 years, now grown old and peevish, had no mind to Work; and being forced into the Wheel by a man whose Business it had been to put him in for the same Space of Time, got out in a Fury, and fasten'd his Teeth in the Calf of the Man's Leg and tore it to pieces. The Man cry'd out but nobody heard him, and the Ass came again and suck'd his Blood, so that he died on Saturday morning. The Ass was shot immediately.

The identity of the donkey keeper is not given, but only one man was buried at St Stephen's in August that year – one John Ivory.

No such drama is known of at Annables in Kinsbourne Green, where Dink the donkey was drawing water from the 145-foot-deep well on a treadmill at a rate of 18 gallons of water in ten to fifteen minutes until close to the end of the nineteenth century. Donkey keeper Thomas Welch died in 1881, when the installation of a pump finally relieved the animal from his duties. The tiled well-house, now listed Grade II, still exists.

Human treadmills were used to supply water for prisons. In St Albans' gaol thirty-two prisoners serving hard labour trod on for twenty minutes and off for ten until the practice was banned in 1902.

A horse mill served the well behind the stables at the late eighteenth century Palladian mansion at Gorhambury. A roofed structure covers the area where a horse circled the well. How the well, still to be seen among the ruins of Sir Nicholas Bacon's Gorhambury, was operated cannot be known, although we know that Tudor house was also served with water piped from the river on the estate by means of a windmill and a donkey's efforts.

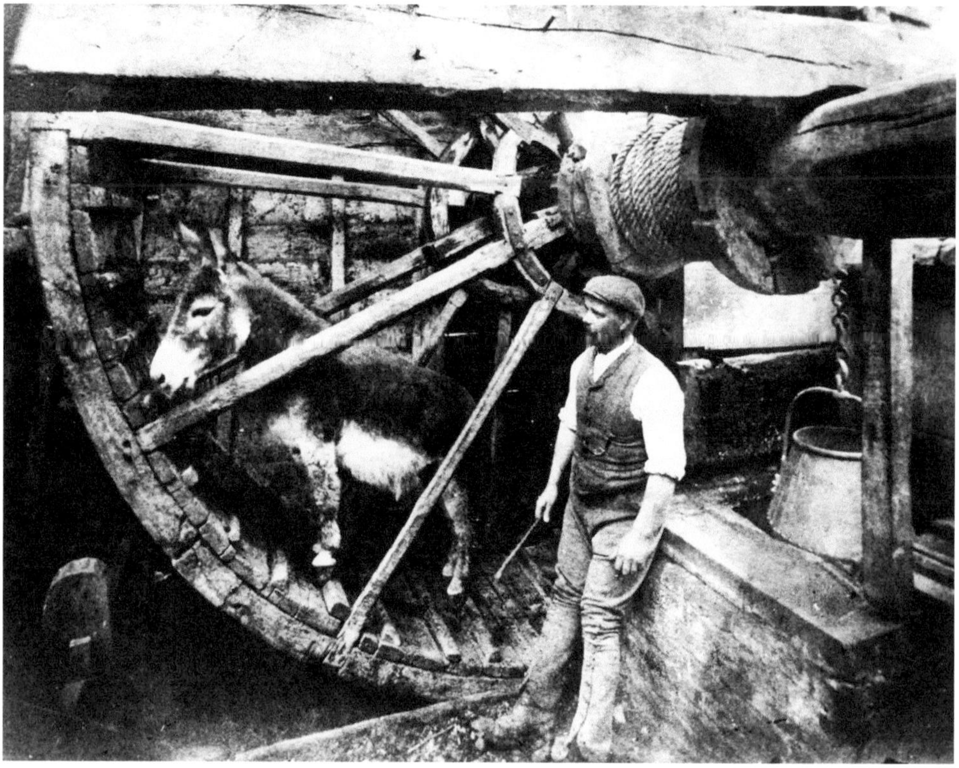

Dink the donkey at the treadmill. Photograph by Frederick Thurston. (Harpenden LHS)

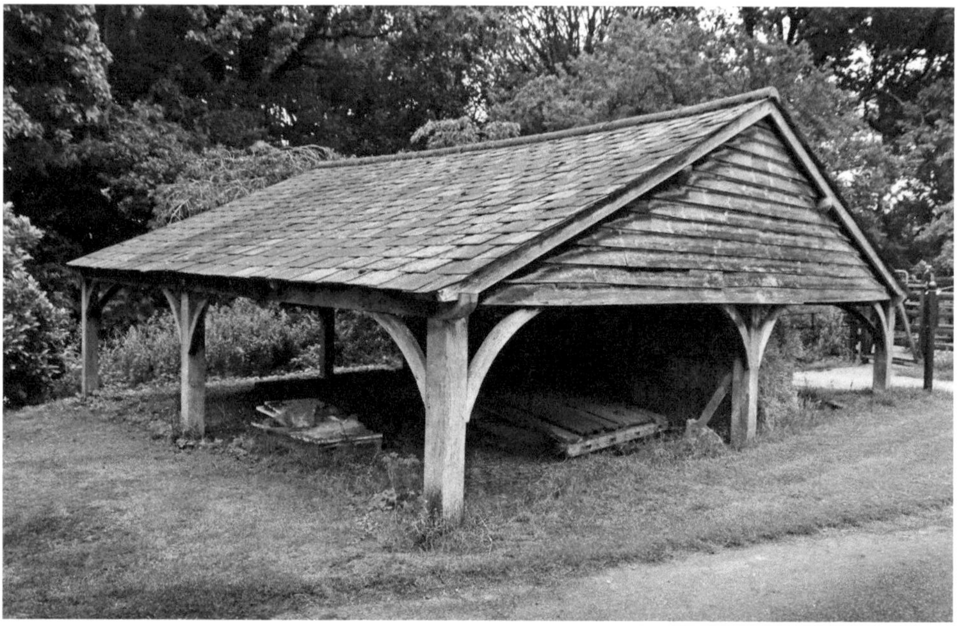

The wellhouse at Gorhambury. (Irina Wright)

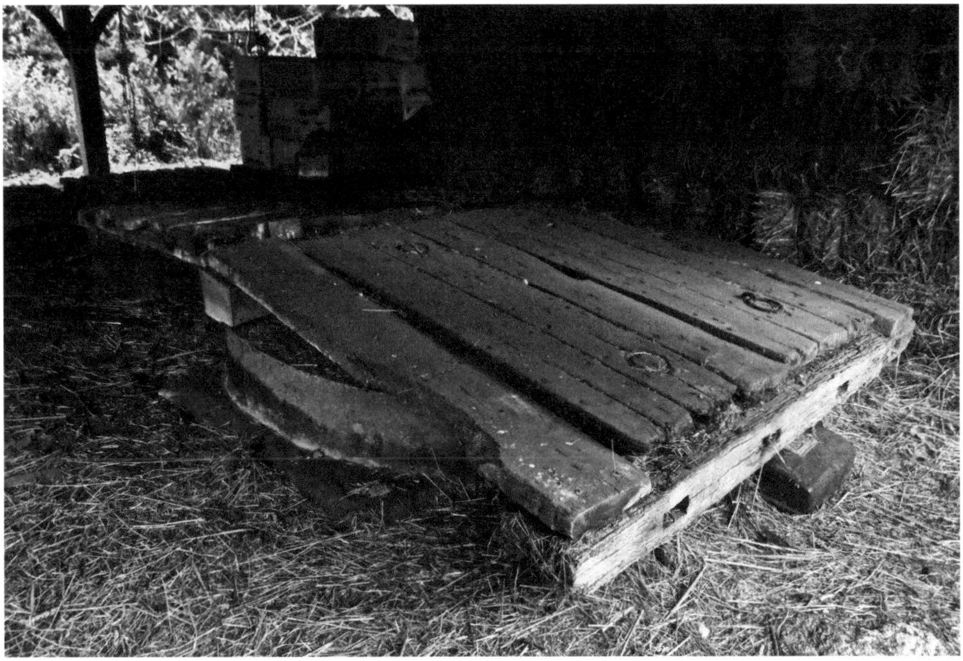

The well at Gorhambury. (Irina Wright)

DID YOU KNOW?

The chalk aquifer of the Chilterns is a geological feature found almost exclusively in North Western Europe. The aquifer holds rainwater which is released through fissures in the rock into the rivers and wells, and sometimes causes springs. The pure water this provides generates a valuable habitat for both wildlife and plants and good well water for communities in the area. The River Ver is such a chalk stream. In times of drought its level can drop, but for centuries it supported corn mills and other industrial activities in St Albans. Deep wells in the town above supplied its houses and inns until piped water was provided from boreholes on Bernards Heath in the nineteenth century.

Some Wells in the Town

Pumps were more in evidence in the urban area, though manpower was no doubt also used. At The Vintry on High Street, built in 1720, there was a well in the service area behind the house. Sale particulars of 1851 describe 'a wellhouse with a double crank forcing pump which supplied the house and also a large rainwater tank completed by the late owner (lawyer and banker John Samuel Story) regardless of expense'. The Vintry is now Côte restaurant.

Revd Robert Rumney's will of 1743 granted the use of his 'recently dug draw well' at his St Peter's Street mansion to his neighbours, provided they behaved themselves 'quietly and inoffensively' and contributed half the costs of maintaining the buckets, chains, gears and house.

Robert Clavering had a single well dug between his two adjoining houses in St Peter's Street. He insured the two properties for £400 in 1738, with his tiled well-house valued at four pounds.

Sharing of wells seems to have been convenient and common and, as early as 1666, John Carter charged his neighbour Edmund How on the corner of George Street and Romeland £72 for the right to draw water from his property. In 1722, widow Elizabeth How, perhaps of the same family, specified her well at the Dog Inn in French Row should continue to be shared with the house next door.

The sale, in 1749, of the Goat Inn on Sopwell Lane by Francis Nicholls and John Christopher Sherman to Archibald Finney included rights and obligations over a nearby well. Use depended on payment of one shilling annually to keep the well, bucket, rope and chain in order.[5]

At The Buildings, the apartments the Duchess of Marlborough erected in the 1730s on Hatfield Road, a well-house stood in the forecourt. Buckler's drawing of 1831 shows it with a large wheel, not unlike that of the Braithwaite pumps elsewhere in the town.

Communal Wells

A communal well might run on subscription. Rent was paid for use of the Counter House well in the 1580s. The Counter House was the gaol, and part of the late sixteenth-century town hall, now W. H. Smith in the Market Place.

St Peter's parish had its own well almost exactly where the war memorial now stands to the south of the church. In the late seventeenth century, Edmund How had a lease on it and was in trouble with the parish vestry for failure to repair it. In 1732 the Corporation stepped in and gave Thomas Gape, one of the borough's two Members of Parliament, leave to clear it out. Gape however died later that year, apparently without issue, and it was his father who paid the twenty pounds for the work, obtaining a ninety-nine-year lease on the well 'next to the house of Adam Munn' at a peppercorn rent.

Since he too died only a year later, it was his grandson, another Thomas, to whom, in 1752, blacksmith Adam Munn was paying one pound for use of the well all year. In 1790 Gape let the well on for the remaining thirty-one years of the original lease to Thomas Lewis, the arrangement to include the shed, bucket and rope. By 1818, Gape's successor, his only surviving son, Revd James Carpenter Gape, no doubt concerned about his continuing responsibility for maintenance, surrendered the lease to the churchwardens, who sought subscriptions for the necessary repairs. It cost £43.7.9 ½ to repair the well, and a new lease was then granted to a Mr Silk, though repairs were to remain the landlord's responsibility and the water supply was to be open to the public.

In 1847, a pump was installed at the well, which served until finally, in 1887, with the arrival of piped water from the new waterworks at Stonecross, the redundant well was filled in and the pump sold.

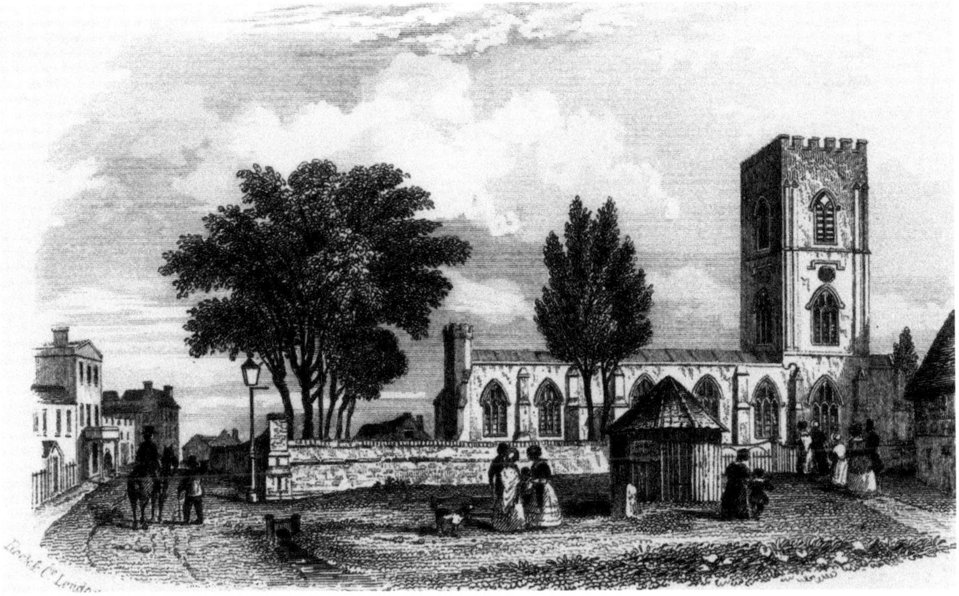

Postcard by Rock & Co. showing St Peter's Wellhouse and the channel bringing water to the Cock Pond, possibly in the 1840s. (SAMS)

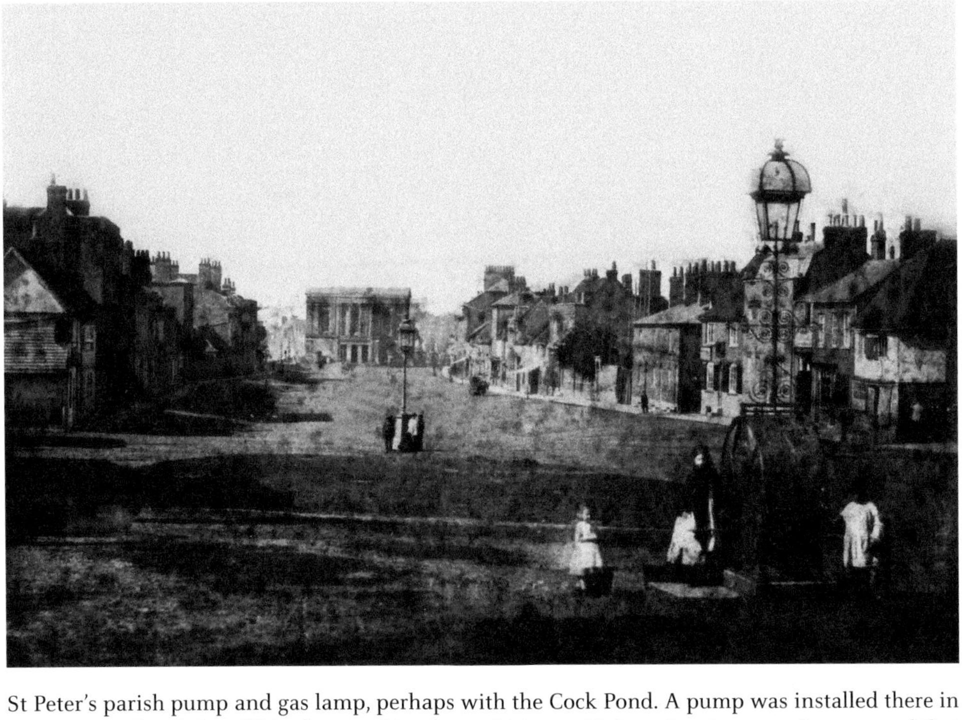

St Peter's parish pump and gas lamp, perhaps with the Cock Pond. A pump was installed there in 1847. It was decided to fill in the pond in 1849, which would date the photograph to around that year, though this could be a replacement by the pump from the Market Place, which was removed in the 1870s. (SAMS)

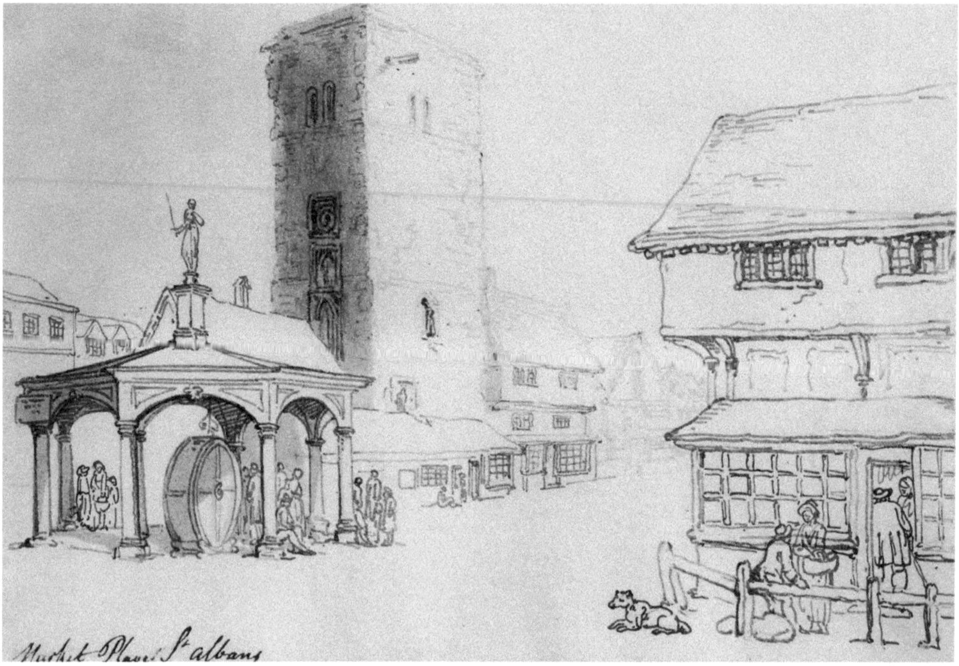

Photographic print of a sketch of the Market Place in 1800, probably by Thomas Rowlandson. (SAMS)

The busy market area had a public water supply at least from 1765 when a pump was installed at the expense of Lord Spencer. The philanthropy was genuine and welcomed by the Corporation, but his generous gifts and loans came at the price of the town's support for his nominees for the town's representation in parliament. Readily given, at the 1761 election the town had returned Spencer's candidate, young George Harcourt, whose father was prominent at court and influential with the king. Ironically, Harcourt's father was, in 1777, to fall into a well whilst rescuing his dog. The dog was found just above the well water on his master's feet, which was all that could be seen of the unfortunate man.

Lord Spencer was later to complain of the Corporation's failure to maintain his pump and a report in the Universal Register of 1786 describes a further installation by John Braithwaite. Of this celebrated engineer of a family of whitesmiths from St Albans, it says,

> this extraordinary genius is very expert at raising water from great depths. He contrived and executed the pump or fountain at St Albans 20 miles from London about four years ago since which it has received no repairs and was never once out of order. The well is near 100 feet from the surface yet a girl of 10 years old pumps the water easily with one hand.

Jacob Schnebbelie's 1787 drawing of the Clock Tower shows a Braithwaite pump under the Market Cross. What is probably the oldest photographic image from St Albans, almost certainly from 1858, also shows a pump, which looks remarkably similar, but surrounded by railings. The Market Cross had been taken down around 1811 following damage by more than one wagon being driven into it, but the pump remained.

Even Braithwaite's pump needed repair eventually and in 1822 the Corporation authorised repairs to the tune of £146.2.0 and in 1833 of a further ten pounds. The pump continued in service until, in 1870, an offer was made by wealthy widow Mrs Isabella Worley to install a drinking fountain in its place. This was not without controversy and some favoured locating this gift in front of the town hall, where another pump had previously stood. As it became clear that Mrs Worley was adamant that her fountain should be in the Market Place facing the High Street, it was even suggested that the old pump should be relocated to the corner of the Clock Tower. After four years of what seems to have been at least prevarication, and perhaps acrimonious debate, an ornate granite fountain to the design of Sir George Gilbert Scott was installed in Mrs Worley's favoured position. It is not clear what happened to the Braithwaite pump, though it is possible that this pump replaced the 1847 pump at St Peter's well, and continued in service there for a dozen or so more years.

Sadly, the fountain obstructed the increasing motorised traffic on the High Street and by the 1920s its days were numbered. Taken apart, it was lost to its original purpose for half a century but is happily now put back together and graces the 1980s office development behind the old Victorian prison building near the City Station.

Another public pump, the Blue Pump, was located on St Peter's Street, in front of the six cottages which were Clark's Almshouses. Both the pump and the almshouses were demolished in 1831 and replaced by the new courtroom and town hall, now the museum and gallery. The pump had been regularly out of action, so was perhaps not missed.

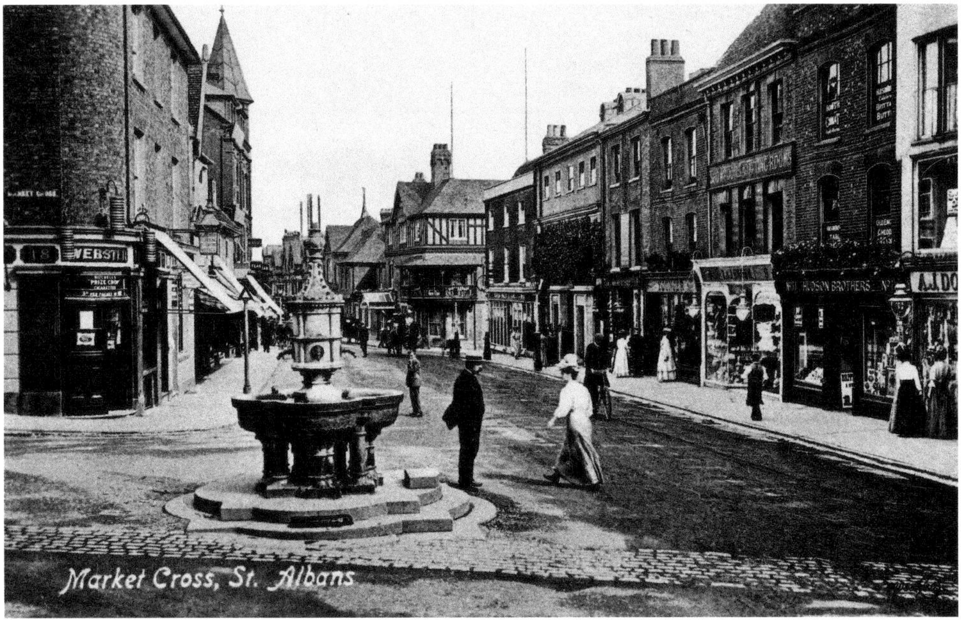

Postcard with Mrs Worley's drinking fountain in the Market Place. (Copyright reserved) (SAMS)

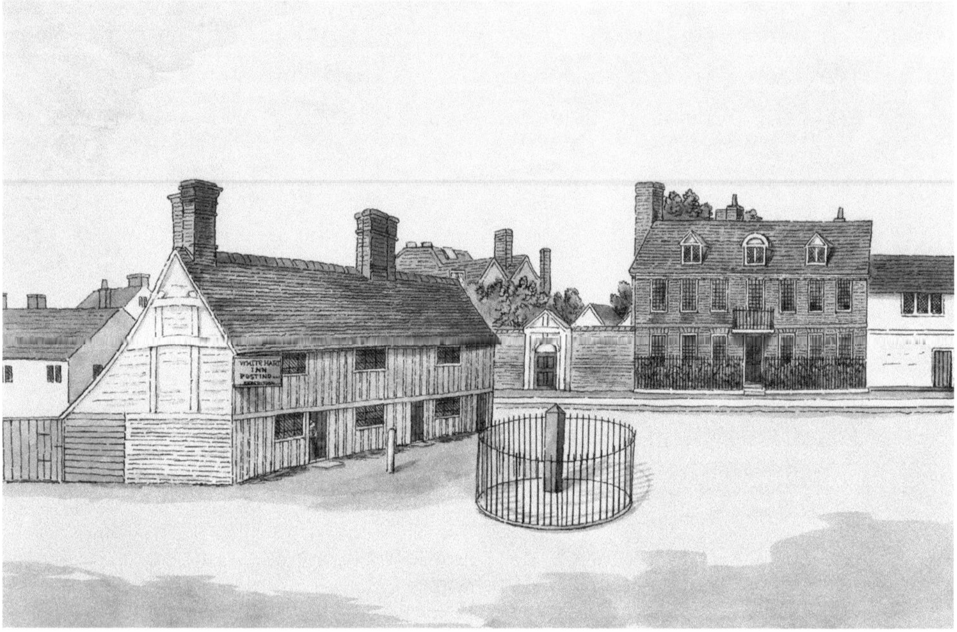

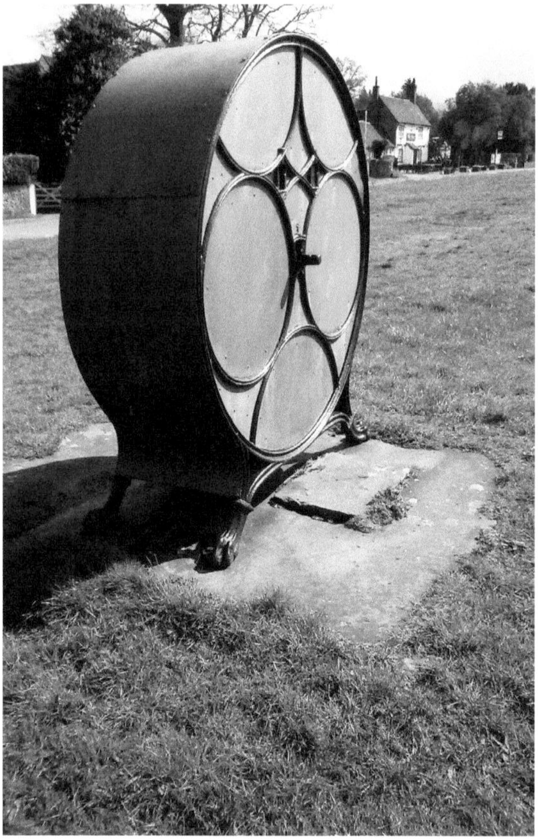

Above: The Blue Pump in front of Clark's Almshouses which stood where the museum and gallery is now. (SAMS)

Left: The Braithwaite pump preserved on the common at Sarratt today. (David Smart)

In 1820, a plumber, John Peele, was gaoled in the Abbey Gatehouse for twelve months for stealing copper pipes and a pump-barrel valued at twenty-five shillings from the Blue Pump. He was caught with the pipes by the toll keeper as he made off to London with his spoils. During improvement works to the town hall in 1899, workmen stumbled on the old well under the building.

Another Braithwaite pump was installed in support of the 245-foot-deep well at Harrow in 1816. The pump had a flywheel and if worked by two youths at their utmost strength, could raise 2.5 gallons of water in thirty seconds, a rate of 300 gallons per hour.[6] A Braithwaite pump at Sarratt still survives on the village green there, though it ceased to be used in the 1920s. A letter to the editor of *Farm and Country* in 1960 shows a photograph of it then, without the safety plate it now wears, and describes its gear wheels and detachable handle.

The Town's Ponds and Cisterns

At least from the seventeenth century there were three ponds in St Peter's Street: Monday's pond or White Horse pond more or less outside present-day Marks and Spencers; Cock, or Lower Cock pond, outside the Cock Inn at the corner of Hatfield Road; and another one, Upper Cock pond, at the top of St Peter's Street in front of 'The Cricketers'.

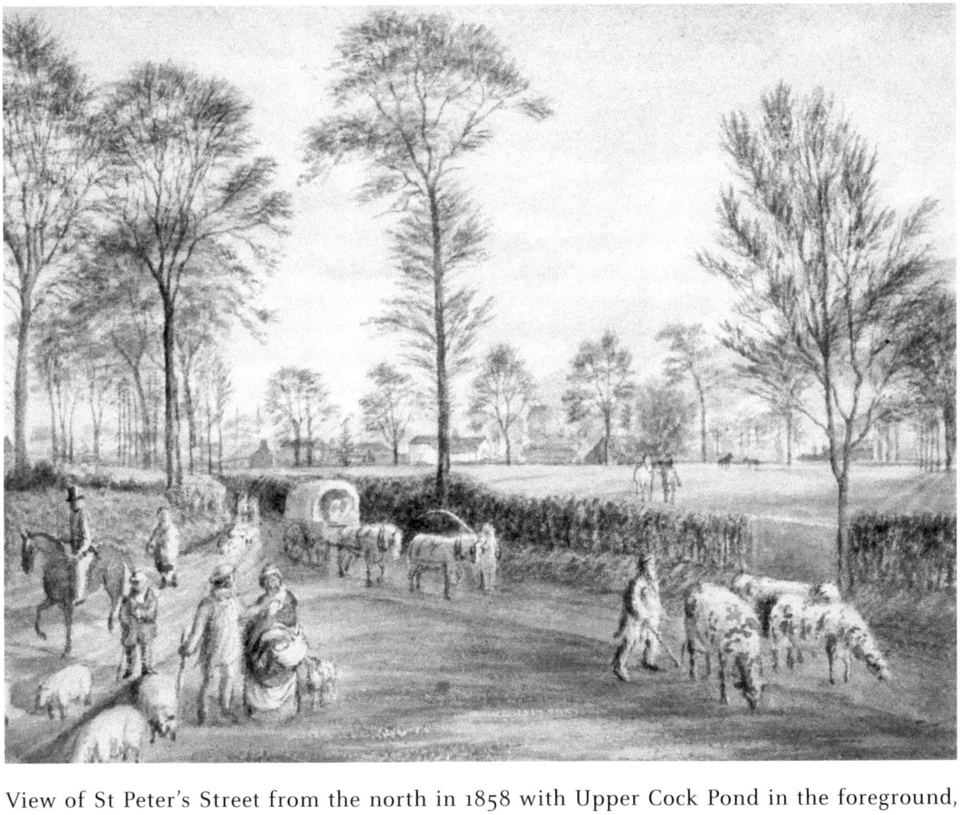

View of St Peter's Street from the north in 1858 with Upper Cock Pond in the foreground, by J. H. Buckingham. (SAMS)

In 1769 St Peter's parish was indicted for nuisance at the Lower Pond. A brick arch was built from the pond to Mrs Mary Mardell's and to the corner of the Revd Mr Boys' dwelling house at a cost of £21.15.11 around that time. Whether this was the solution to the problem, or had caused it, was not explained. A similar causeway was built from the vicarage to St Peter's Church opposite over the flow of water from Bernards Heath.

The St Albans ponds were farmed, or leased, generally to aldermen of the town. In 1713 the twenty-one-year lease of Cock Pond was charged at four pence per annum, with the obligation to rail it and maintain it. In 1739 both ponds were let on a similar basis but for a single year and at only one penny per annum.

Maintenance of the ponds was a continuing problem, and on 9 August 1800 John Carrington of Bramfield observed that all three ponds were dry and cleaned out. By 1824 the Corporation was seeking a public subscription for the task of filling in the White Horse pond and replacing it with a covered tank to hold water in case of fire, but a year later the decision was taken to deepen the Cock pond and dispense with the tank at the White Horse.

By 1835 St Peter's Vestry was considering filling in the Upper Cock pond and the ditch which fed it. They favoured instead an open pebbled channel on the side of the road opposite the Sailor Boy (now the Jolly Sailor) which would bring water down to the now deepened Cock pond. However, even this pond was filled in in 1849, when piped water became available to subscribing households, in communal yards, and presumably to the fire service.

Piped Water for the Town

The nineteenth-century waterworks on Bernards Heath were not the first attempt to provide piped water in the town. In the 1690s, a John Green, prompted by Walter Whitfeild, who had served with the (then) Earl Marlborough and enjoyed his patronage, obtained a ninety-nine-year lease as from the mayor and Corporation by the town clerk, Thomas Richards, to provide wholesome water to the town from a site on the Holywell River, undertaking to make good any damage which occurred as a result. This refers to the section of the Ver which passed through the earl's garden at Holywell House, then being developed in the fashionable Dutch style with canals and other water features.

The height of the town above the river, and pollution of the river water by the tanners made it an unlikely exercise. The many wells provided good water direct from the aquifer, but it did come to fruition for a few decades.

No suitable site for the works could be found and Green was no engineer, so Whitfeild took over the lease, giving shares to a Richard Barry and to Richards, though Barry soon sold his shares on to water engineer and King's Hydrographer Thomas Tuttell. Richards was acting without authority and Tuttell's share was never acknowledged. Instead yet another lease was granted by Richards to the well-known plumber William Yarnold, who set up the waterworks on the river at Sopwell. Elm pipes were laid up to what is now Marlborough Road, the line of the old Tonman Ditch, the eastern boundary of the town. This route was to minimise disruption to the traffic in the town. The water was pumped up to cisterns on Cock Lane, now Hatfield Road. On completion of the work, Yarnold sold his lease for a handsome profit, and moved on. Whitfeild sued for his hoped-for

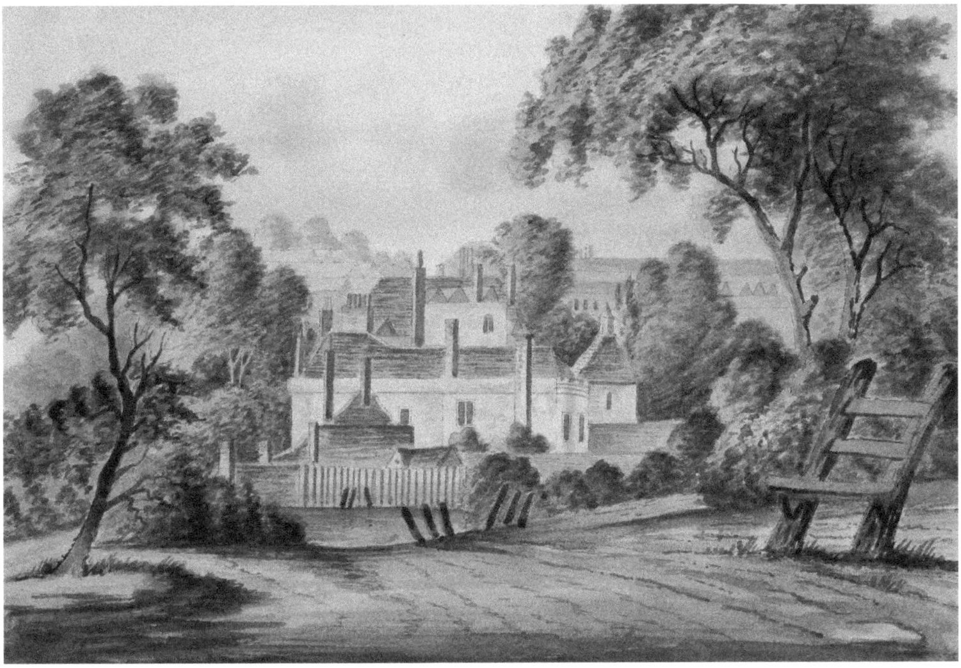

Copy by H. R. Wilton Hall of a drawing of Holywell House from St Stephen's Hill in the 1790s by Thomas Baskerfield. (SAMS)

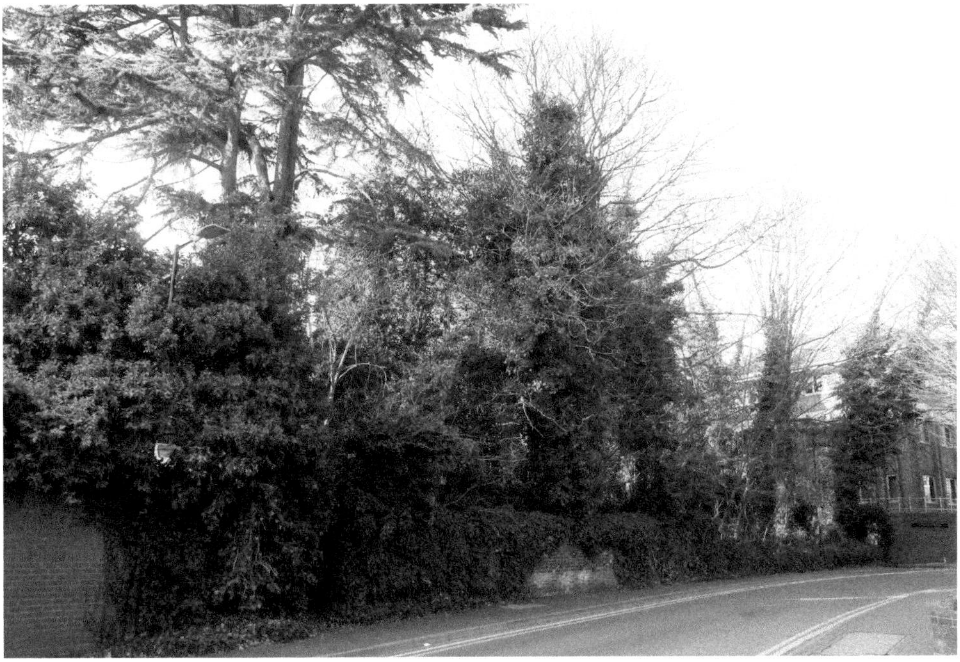

The only remaining evidence of the ancient Tonman Ditch on Upper Marlborough Road. (Kari Lundgaard)

25 per cent of the return and Tuttell for compensation for his unrecognised share. The mayor was less than interested and Richards absconded, apparently jumping before he was pushed by the Corporation.

This litigation, stored in the National Archives, reveals the story of this rather bizarre episode in the town's history.[7] Tuttell died in 1702 whilst surveying the Thames, without having succeeded in his case, but his deposition explains that he would not have pumped water from the polluted river but from boreholes, which the townspeople were already in effect doing individually. The lease finished up in the hands of James Bennett, steward to Sir Samuel Grimston of Gorhambury. Bennett already occupied the house at Sopwell, which had belonged to Grimstons since 1669, and in 1698 Grimston granted Bennett the freehold of the waterworks site. Bennett sold his interest in the St Albans enterprise on in 1720 to John Walton and John Hall, who distributed 600 shares to interested parties.[8] Well-known local names appear as shareholders, but also some London men. It is not clear how long the enterprise lasted, but perhaps a further ten years.

The waterworks are shown on the Andrews and Wren plan of the town printed in 1766 but we know that by 1764 Henry Potter was using the site for his London-based diamond polishing business. With Potter in financial difficulties by the late 1770s, there was an attempt to re-establish the waterworks by a John Stirling, probably the energetic

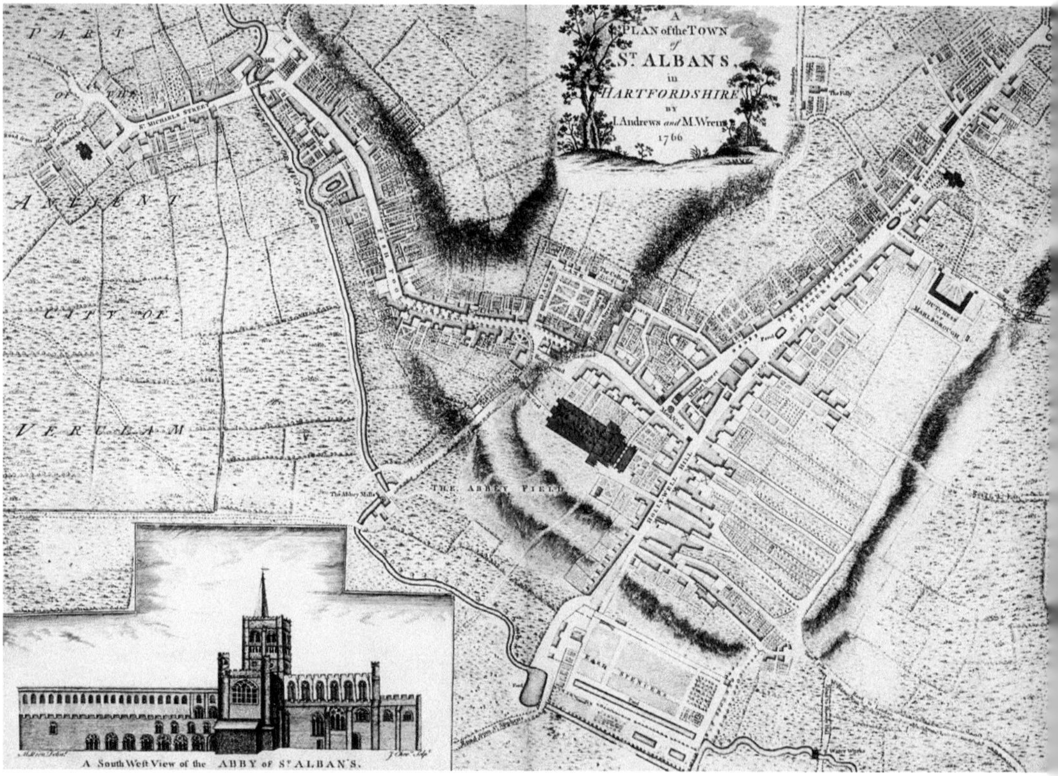

Plan of the town drawn by Andrews and Wren. (SAMS)

textile entrepreneur who also brought water supply to Glasgow. He was the son of Alexander Stirling, who had been mayor of St Albans earlier, and he and his parents struck a deal in 1777 to acquire the site. However, nothing came of the plan and following Potter's complete demise in 1779 the site was taken up by others who built a brand-new mill on the site for the production of cotton candlewick.

The Town's Nineteenth-century Waterworks

It was brick-maker and builder Joseph Fowler who first attempted to supply piped water from Bernards Heath. However, he died in 1834 leaving debts of £1,700 to iron merchant Bowman for supply of his engine and the pipes. In 1835 millwright George Blaxland came to continue the enterprise there, taking a lease on an acre of land on the Townsend side of the Heath, where he built a house, now known as Heath House, and workshops, but this operation too was short-lived. Unable to service his loans from George Alfred Muskett, banker and MP for St Albans, he left to take up a post as chief engineer to the Commercial Steam Packet Company. The list of his assets as he relinquished the lease included his kitchen range and dressers in the house, a steam engine, a screwing machine, bellows, five anvils, two furnaces and apparatus, two turning lathes with screwing apparatus attached, and some shafting and pulleys.

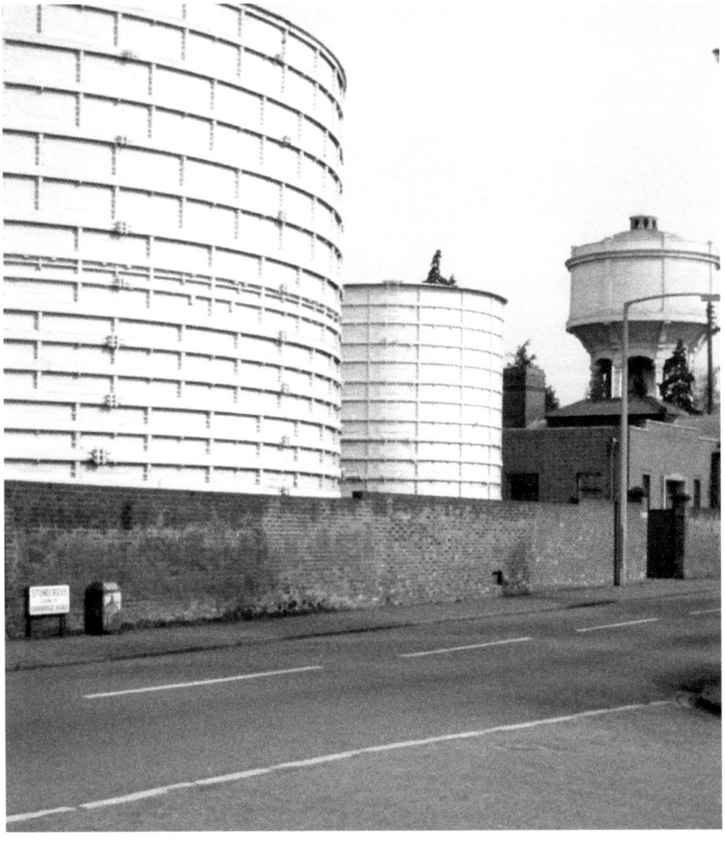

The water towers at Stonecross taken in 1968 by Alf Gentle. (SAMS)

There continued to be waterworks on this part of the Heath, recorded at the time of the Tithe Commutation in 1843 as in the occupancy of a John Oakes. In 1854 the brothers Thomas Haden and James Oakes, substantial Derbyshire coal and ironmasters, acquired the lands at Snatchup to build new works later to be incorporated as the St Albans Water Company. The price of this supply could not be afforded by the humbler residents of the town and drawing water at the standpipes without payment was the subject of prosecutions. Powerful pumps still provide some of our tap water from deep boreholes and reservoirs there today; the engine room and manager's house still exist, but as offices, though the original cast-iron water towers and reinforced concrete one added around 1913, which many will remember, were both demolished some time ago.

The River Ver Today

The river itself no longer sustains any industry, though some of the mills still exist and there are still traces of the watercress beds that thrived in the nineteenth century. As that industry waned the disused beds became derelict and the adjacent land used for allotments and scrap storage. In 1992 the Watercress Wildlife Association was formed and now maintains the area where the Sopwell beds were. Accessible from the end of Riverside Road, the reserve provides a peaceful haven for wildlife and visitors.

The Ver Valley Society, formed in 1976, acts as watchdog for the conservation of the river and provides illustrated leaflets for walks along its banks. In 1970 the mill at

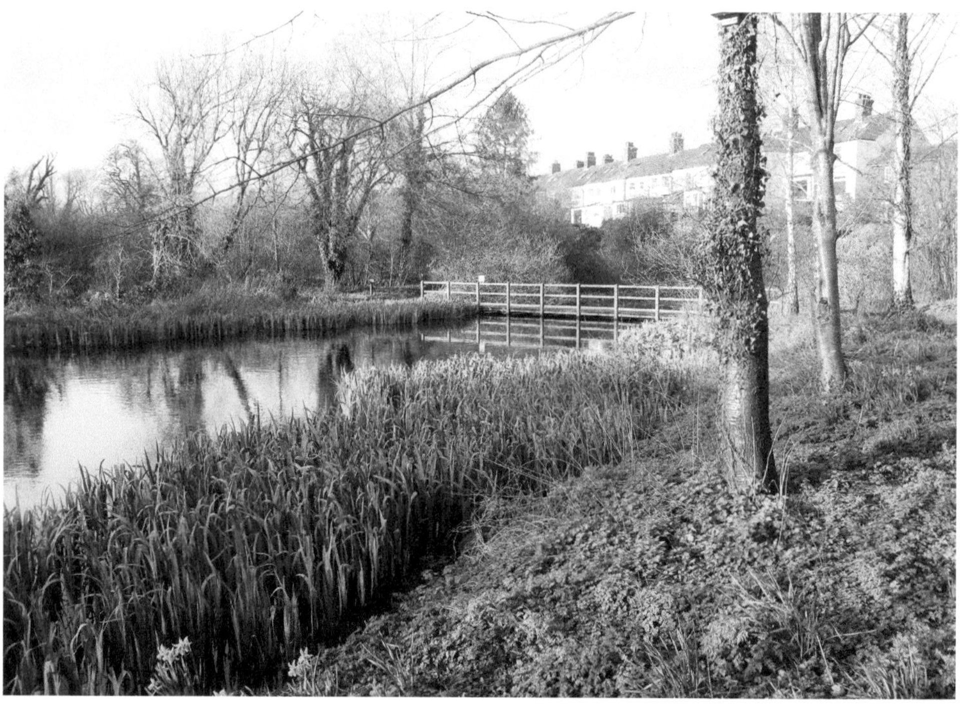

The beautiful Watercress Wildlife Association reserve to the rear of houses on Riverside Road. (Kari Lundgaard)

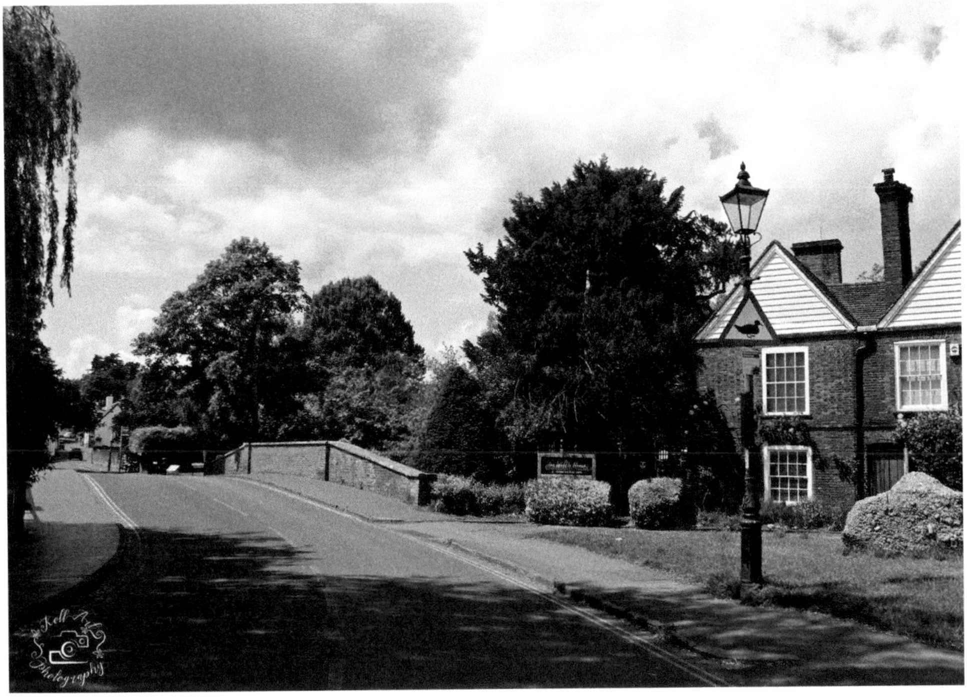

The Waffle House restaurant beside the bridge at St Michael's. (Koll-Art Photography)

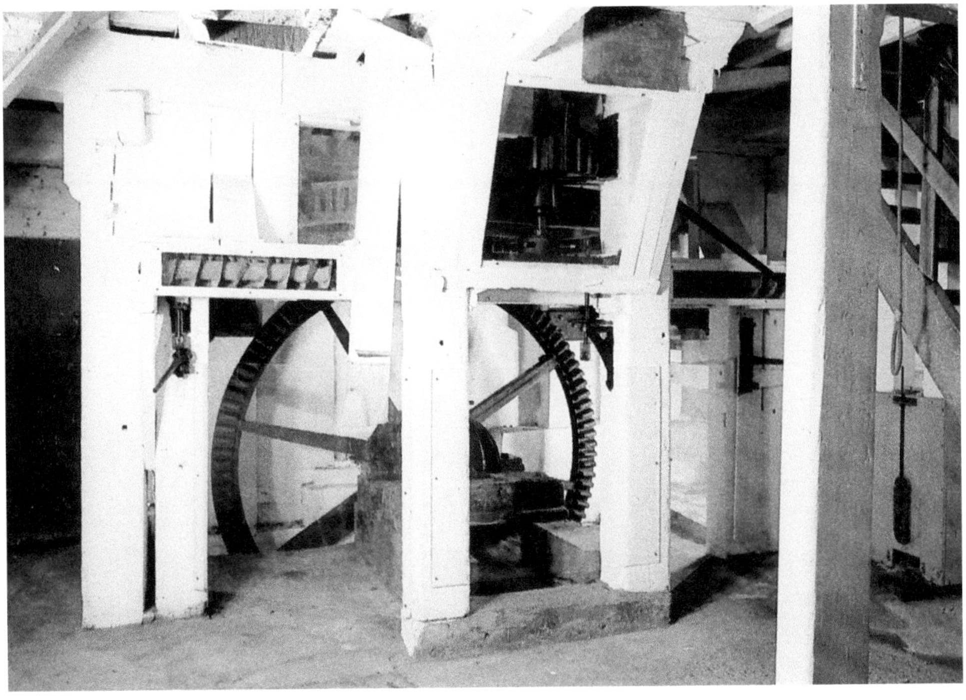

Postcard showing the mill wheel at Kingsbury. (Copyright reserved)

Kingsbury was opened as a museum with the old equipment a reminder of the industries of the past, but, though the mill wheel is still there, it is now inside the very popular Waffle House restaurant.

Twentieth-century demands for water have meant that there has been abstraction from the aquifer. The pumping of water further north for both industry and consumers, and the consequent reduction of water levels downstream near to St Albans, has remained a controversial issue. Though water is no longer needed for power, nor for the tanning of leather, this reduction does have consequences as it alters the habitat which the chalk stream offers both flora and fauna.

4. Birth, Death and the Married State

Until civil registration, introduced in 1837, baptisms, marriages and burials were recorded exclusively by the clergy. The parish registers of the Abbey parish, and St Peter's and St Michael's, are the principal source of information on who was born, married or was buried in St Albans, though nonconformists also kept records for their own communities.

Baptisms would generally reflect the number of children born in a town, but marriage and burial records are less representative. Many of the less well-off did not marry; many, being widowed, married twice or more; and many married away from their own parish. The Abbey Church attracted many weddings from elsewhere. Burials might have included visitors dying here, whilst those dying whilst away could be buried at their place of death.

In 1783, in order to pay for the American War of Independence, George III introduced an unpopular stamp duty.[9] Three pence was charged for each baptismal, marriage and burial record, with a five pound fine for refusal to pay. Vicars were to receive 10 per cent of the takings for their trouble in collecting this. Paupers (those 'on the parish') were not charged and exempt entries were marked accordingly. St Peter's vicar, Thomas D'Oyly, perhaps sympathetic towards his flock, marked twenty-two of the thirty-seven burials that year as exempt. The high number could reflect the age and level of parish dependency of the deceased, though strangely none were so marked in the Abbey parish.

Birth

During the eighteenth century, each community would have a midwife who took care of the very frequent births in every household, sometimes acting witness in cases where proof of birth to a particular woman was needed, but it then became fashionable for ladies to employ the services of surgeons, notably in St Albans, Joseph Handley, now advertising as man-midwives. In the event of difficult births, or other special cases, baptisms could take place in the home, but would still appear in the registers. Hazardous enough, birth was only the first hurdle in a child's life. The rate of child mortality was very high.

Marriage

Until Hardwicke's Marriage Act of 1753, couples could, with a licence, be married by any clergyman, anywhere. This could allow privacy and circumvention of any risk of family disapproval. However, the new law required parental consent for minors and marriage ceremonies to take place in the parish of either bride or groom. This brought better records of marriage, though as the Act did not apply in Scotland, runaway marriages to Gretna Green became common. Marriage settlements between families, or arranged marriages, were little affected, but for some there was less inclination to marry at all.

The potential disinclination to marry was of concern to the ladies of St Albans, who, on the marriage of George III in 1761, wrote to the royal couple to express their pleasure at the example they set for the nation. This was soon followed by some wag petitioning the newly-wed Queen, supposedly on behalf of maidens of thirty years of age and upwards, for a tax on bachelors 'to be appropriated to the support of neglected and superannuated virgins'. Though not imposed then, it has in fact not been uncommon for such a 'bachelor tax' to be proposed, including during the Second World War II in 1941.[10]

To the Queen's most excellent Majesty.

The humble Address of the ladies of the borough of St. Albans, in the county of Hertford.

May it please your majesty, we your most dutiful and affectionate subjects, being by custom precluded from being named in the address of the mayor and corporation of this place, beg leave to approach your majesty with the warmest congratulations on your happy nuptials. Formed by nature, and improved by the completest education, you were selected by the best of kings, to add the only happiness that was wanting to his majesty in this world. As subjects are greatly influenced by the example of their sovereign, we have the greatest reason to hope that the matrimonial state will be duly honoured by your majesty's dutiful subjects cheerfully following the royal example : an example too much wanted in this degenerate age, wherein that happy state to which we all aspire, and the sweets of which you have now enjoyed, is made the object of ridicule instead of respect, by too many vain, giddy, and dissipated minds. If the riches of a nation consist in its populousness, this happy country will, in this respect, too soon become poor, whilst the lawful means to continue posterity are either shackled by the restraints of mistaken laws, or despised by those who respect none. But as every virtuous and commendable action is encouraged by your royal consort, and your own noble sentiments and conduct, we hope this example will be duly followed by your majesty's loyal subjects. That you may long remain a pattern of conjugal fidelity and happiness, and see a numerous offspring grow up as tender plants under your maternal influence, to be a blessing to their royal parents and to this nation, are the sincere and ardent wishes of your majesty's most dutiful and devoted subjects,

The Ladies of St. Albans

In 1760 there had been thirty-two marriages in the town at the Abbey Church and St Peter's, but only twenty-four in 1761. This rose again to thirty-three in 1762, though the increase that year cannot be regarded as significant with such a small sample!

Divorce

Marriage was a commitment for life and until the Matrimonial Causes Act of 1857 divorce and remarriage was only possible by annulment or costly Private Act of Parliament.

A successful suit in the ecclesiastical courts for separation of bed and board on grounds of adultery gave freedom but no right to remarry. This was relatively common, but there were few Private Acts. It was usually the husband who undertook the suit and some did so with no view to actual separation, but only either to bring an errant wife to heel, or claim substantial damages from the wife's lover.

In 1768, the Baron Grosvenor, though hugely rich, did not bother to seek a divorce from his wife Henrietta following their separation. It would, in any event, have been capable of challenge on account of his own infidelity with prostitutes. Her misdemeanor was an affair with Prince Henry, Duke of Cumberland, at the White Hart Inn on Holywell Hill, for which Grosvenor claimed damages of £10,000 and £3,000 costs. Unable to pay, Henry had to seek the money from the Civil List. With it, Grosvenor granted Henrietta an allowance of £1,200 per annum and continued his own promiscuous lifestyle.

The White Hart had been convenient for Henry and Henrietta. He could join her there, from London, on her journeys to and from the Grosvenor family estates in Cheshire. His incognito was the dress of a common farmer, but this was quickly cracked by the lady's servants, who soon connived with landlady Mrs Langford to reveal all.

Two other St Albans cases involved the dalliance of married ladies with dashing young men either going to or returning from service with the East India Company. Untimely death followed the one and bankruptcy the other.

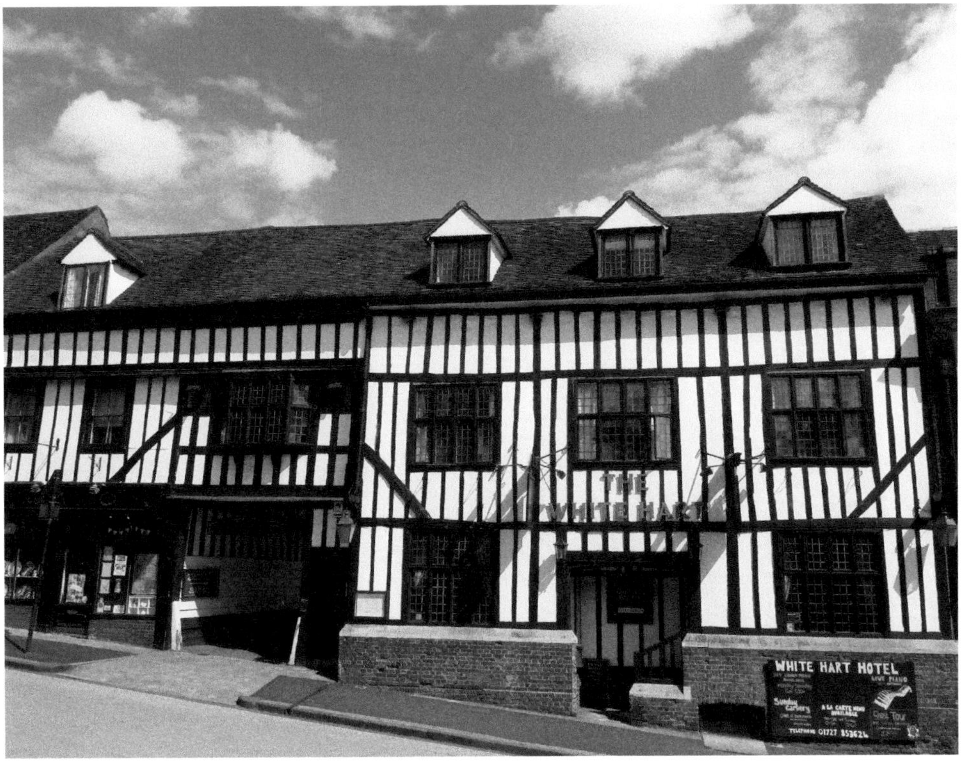

The White Hart Inn on Holywell Hill. (Kari Lundgaard)

Betsy Hodges Handley and George Borradale

In 1765 Dr Joseph Handley arranged the marriage of his only daughter, twenty-two-year-old Betsy Hodges, with George, the only surviving son of Jasper Arris Borradale, of Hall Place. Both fathers were aldermen in the town and the marriage settlement was generous: Jasper made all his St Albans land over to the thirty-three-year-old George, retaining only his home for his lifetime. Handley also committed property.

The marriage was at St Paul's, Covent Garden, where Borradale also had property. Soon a son was born, but only a year later, George was suing Betsy for separation on grounds of adultery with the young son of London jeweller James Bellis. The Bellis family home was at Woodside, near Hatfield, but the business was first in Covent Garden and then Pall Mall.

Betsy was clearly unhappy with married life. On return from a visit to Suffolk, George had booked to stop over at the Rainbow in Fleet Street, a well-known coffee house frequented by theatregoers. Betsy and George's sister, Teresa, declined to join him there and arranged to stay with Bellis. Since the Bellis daughter was already giving up her room for them, there was no room for George. On joining George for the journey back to St Albans, Teresa had to tell him that Betsy had left the house with her trunk, leaving no note of her intended whereabouts. Evidence given later by landlord John Drysdale and his servant revealed that she had stayed some days at his London hotel, a bagnio in Orange Street, together with seventeen-year-old Francis William, the Bellis son.

George had found her there, but she had refused to return to St Albans with him, telling staff that she had run away from him. The young Bellis then took lodgings for her at Wine Office Court in Fleet Street. The landlord's evidence to the court was that although Bellis had said the room was just for Betsy, the young man had indeed spent at least one night with her there. George did bring his wife back to St Albans, leaving her with her father there, but the determined lady returned to London in a post chaise.

The sentence of the court was that 'being altogether unmindful of her conjugal vow' Betsy 'did commit the crime of adultery with the said Francis William Bellis, and did thereby violate her conjugal duty'... 'and the said Revd George Borradale ought by law to be divorced and separated from bed, board and mutual cohabitation with the said Betsy Hodges Borradale'.

George enjoyed his freedom for only two years before his death at only thirty-seven years of age. He was buried at St Peter's on 11 December 1769. Bellis in the meantime was serving in the Infantry for the East India Company in Bombay. In February 1771, he requested return to England to adjust some private affairs which required his personal attendance. He resigned his commission with the option to return without prejudice to his rank. But later that year Betsy married the recently widowed flamboyant King's Proctor, Philip Champion de Crespigny. Bellis sought permission to return to India – perhaps he had had in mind returning with Betsy – but did not go on account of severe illness for which his physician recommended residence in France, saying he should on no account return to a hot climate. Only in 1778 did he resume his career in India. De Crespigny bought the estate at Colney House, just south of St Albans and a boy, Charles, was born to the couple and baptised on 1 June 1772, but sadly Betsy did not survive the birth. Charles survived little longer and was buried in his grandfather Handley's vault in the north transept of the Abbey Church in St Albans in 1774.

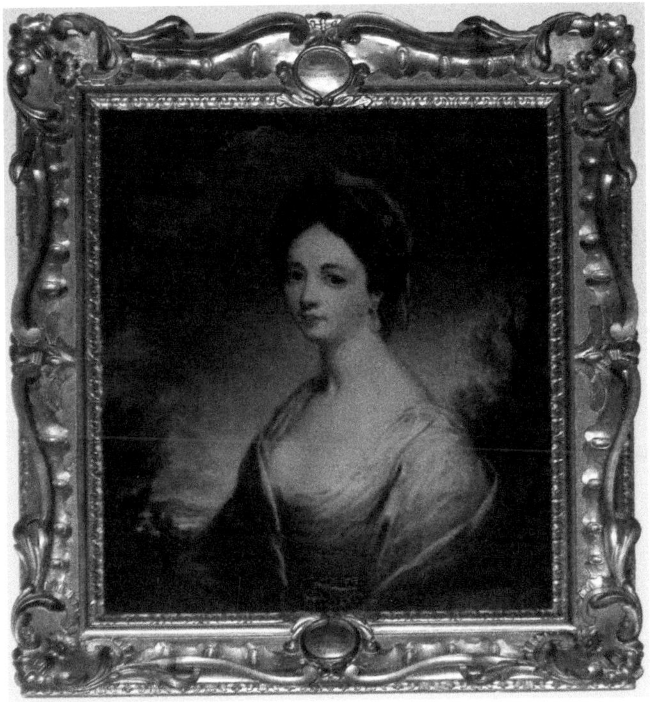

Betsy Hodges de Crespigny. Photographic reproduction of a portrait held at Kelmarsh Hall. (David Smart and Malcolm Merrick)

DID YOU KNOW?

Until 1832, the penalty for forgery was execution. Henry Fauntleroy forged powers of attorney for bonds and stocks lodged with his bank, including those of Francis William Bellis, sometime lover of Betsy Hodges Handley from St Albans. He was executed outside Newgate Prison in 1824.

Ensign Bellis married in India, though his wife died soon after the marriage. He requested retirement on half pay as Lieutenant Colonel in 1800 on account of a liver condition and returned to live in Oxted in Surrey, marrying for the second time in 1810.

Betsy's divorce was written up in a series recording notorious divorces, so we know every detail.[11] Bellis also claimed fame, but posthumously. In 1824, his widow Susannah claimed her inheritance of stocks held in trust at Marsh Sibbald Bank. However, banker Henry Fauntleroy, facing serious financial problems, had sold the stocks over forged signatures. His trial for fraud and subsequent execution outside Newgate Prison, it is said, attracted an audience of 100,000. Following the execution some coins went into circulation with an over-stamped message that read 'Fauntleroy the Robber of Widows and Orphans, Executed at Newgate, such be the Fate of the Insolvent Bilking Bankers and Agents'. One of these coins, with a face value of one penny, sold at auction in 2011 for £47.2.00.

Mary Brideoake and John Samuel Story

Attorney, Alderman John Samuel Story, took his wife to court for her behaviour in the 1830s. Another marriage which had involved a substantial financial settlement, the lady had been caught in flagrante delicto with her husband's nephew, a young man newly returned from adventures in India. It isn't clear whether Story sought an actual separation, but it seems likely he just wanted to make a point. However, his wife was able to prolong the suit by lengthy appeals, such that the alimony, payable until she was proven guilty, together with fees, cost Story his considerable fortune and he, like Borradale, died only shortly after the conclusion of the case, but bankrupt.

Wife-selling

It was, of course, not open to ordinary folk to fund such cases, but there was another solution open to determined separators. The husband could put his wife up for sale, expecting purchase by the co-respondent. A St Albans man named Faulkner offered his wife for sale in the Market Place in 1834 for two shillings and six pence. The practice was frowned upon and not common by this date and the magistrates offered Faulkner bail to keep the peace at one pound, or be sent to prison for violation of public decency.

Treatment of Misdemeanors

Rape was a crime then as now and treated seriously. In 1797 James George McGee was convicted at the Liberty Sessions[12] for committing a rape on Elizabeth Treader. He was ordered to be 'flogged at the cart's tail through all the public streets in St Albans'.[13] This meant being stripped to the waist, tied to the back of a cart and forced to walk behind it as he was whipped.

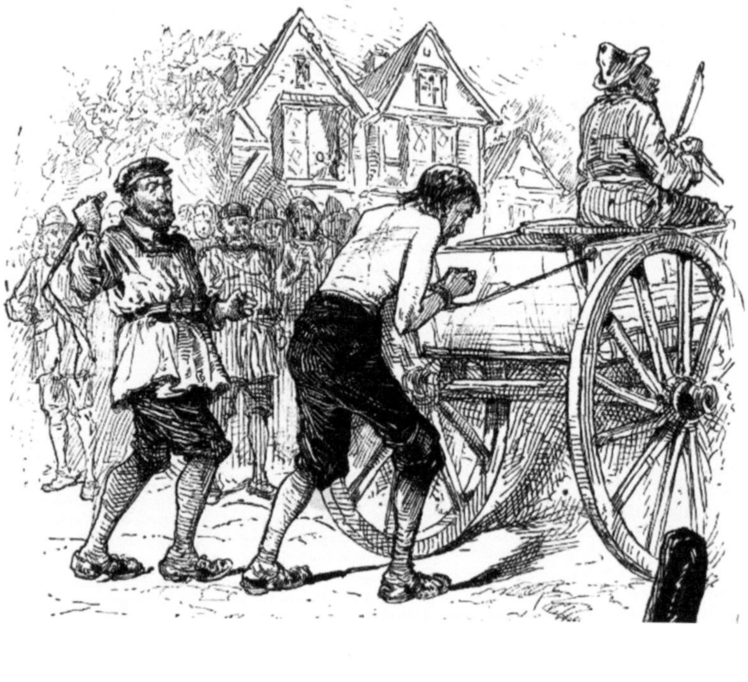

Whipped at the cart's tail – from *The Prince and the Pauper* by Mark Twain. (Project Gutenberg Ebook 1837, sourced 18 February 2020)

The ecclesiastical courts were, until the twentieth century, responsible for matters of decency. In 1747 Archdeacon Cole arbitrated between Archibald Finney of the Great Red Lion and George Makeham, landlord of the Goat, over an alleged debt.[14] Alderman Galbraith said Makeham called Finney 'Gambler and Cheat' and 'having lived by cheating for twenty years', whilst Alderman Firth said Makeham was the aggressor. Francis Niccoll said Makeham had called Finney 'Irish Dog'. Cole concluded there was fault on both sides but that neither intended damaging the public credit of the other. Costs of three pounds five shillings were awarded against Finney, which Makeham should reimburse.

The problem of sexual abuse and human trafficking is an age old one. Hogarth's 'Harlot's Progress' series of 1732 aptly describes the vulnerability of young women in London. Seventeen-year-old Ann Higden, daughter of a millwright in Sopwell Lane, worked at the cotton mill. Ann's mother would use harsh words, and in 1827, Ann ran from this in distress. She sought work at the Lewisham cotton mill, but though the kindly manager could offer none, he gave her two shillings to tide her over. Returning to London and having spent all her money, the unfortunate girl obtained a recommendation for cheap lodgings of an elderly gentleman. A watchman overheard this apparently innocent

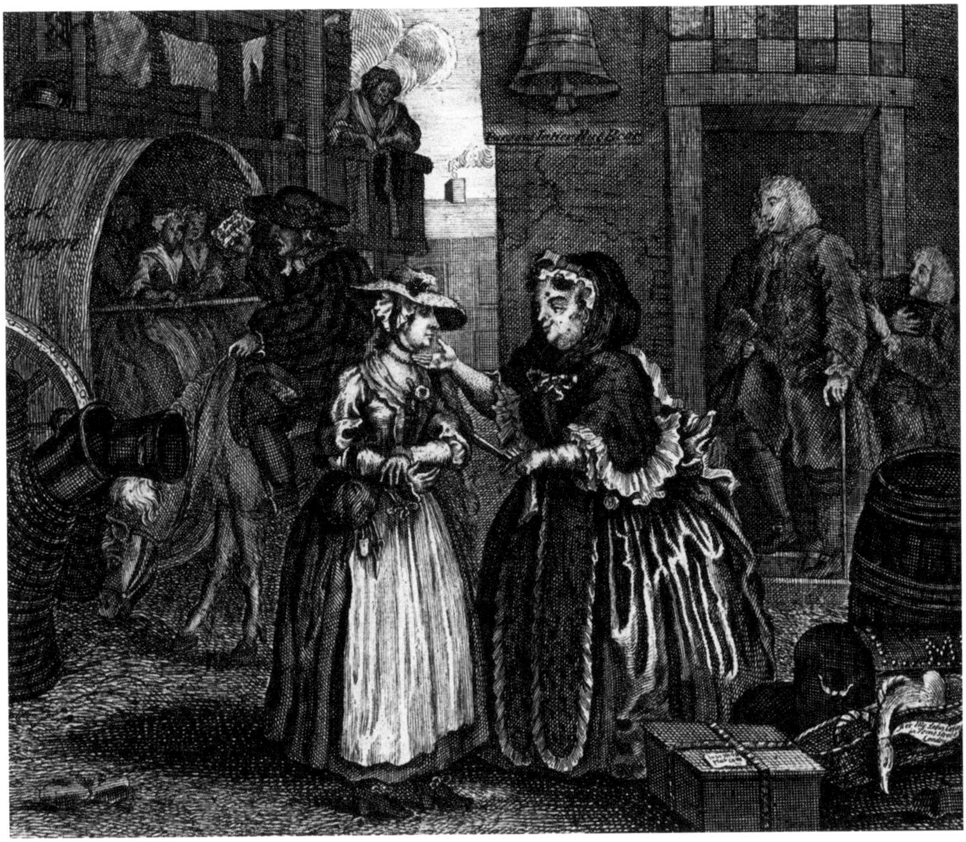

The first in William Hogarth's series of engravings 'The Harlot's Progress', from the 1848 edition of Joseph Gay's *Lure of Venus* held in the British Library.

country girl ask directions to the house in King's Head Court, Shoe Lane. Knowing it to be the address of a house of ill repute, he accompanied her, to find the old man emerging from an alley, clearly with vile intentions. The watchman took the girl and locked her in the Compter for her own safety. The next day, Alderman Birch ordered her return to her family, declaring the girl had narrowly escaped a fate worse than death and praising the foresight of the watchman in rescuing her. Her relieved parents said she had been missing for a week.

Death and Burial

Death in the eighteenth century was often recorded as by Act of God, of an apoplectic fit, or even of a decline, but actual causes of death were often diseases such as smallpox, cholera and typhoid. In 1760 there were fifteen burials at St Stephen's due to smallpox. The Abbey register of 1816 recorded four burials on the same day due to measles. In 1833 a flu epidemic raged in St Albans. Child mortality was particularly high that year, though no burials are recorded as specifically due to the infection. Close to 50 per cent of the 190 burials in the town that year were minors, most under ten years of age. However, ten were over eighty years of age, so longevity, once childhood was survived, was not unusual. The well-to-do were not exempt from such childhood tragedies. Sarah, Duchess of Marlborough lost her only surviving son to smallpox at sixteen years of age in 1703.

Cremation was almost unknown in England until the twentieth century, so burial was the norm. Until the mid-nineteenth century, for the rich, it was often inside their parish church, and in St Albans the Abbey Church hosted most of the local great and good as well as many from farther afield. During the eighteenth century it became common also to erect memorial stones in the churchyards. Parish clergy had traditionally enjoyed the right of grazing their cattle or sheep there, often bemoaning the inconvenient habit of friends and families of the dead of strewing flowers and memorabilia on graves there; however the increasing number of burials restricted that practice and St Peter's Vestry ordered that vicar Revd Thomas D'Oyly should no longer graze his cattle in their churchyard.

Burial was usually very soon after death, though surgeon James Handley, father of Joseph mentioned elsewhere, requested burial to be only one week after his demise 'unless putrefaction should dictate otherwise'. The possibility of burial of an unconscious body before life had completely left it was clearly real. The will of Ann, the widow of Revd William Marston, former vicar of St Michael's, written in 1755, determined there should be no 'fastnings' to her coffin lid nor vault till one full month next after her decease. Shrouds were, by law, made of woollen cloth and the officiating clergyman was obliged to certify that this was done. The five pound penalty for non-compliance was, however, insignificant for those who had other ideas about their final outfits. Ann Topham of New House, now Darrowfield, in St Michael's, left money for the fine in order to be buried in linen. Funerals could be elaborate community events, though it was uncommon for women to attend.

The burials of paupers, or those 'on the parish', was the responsibility of the community, and taken seriously, with suitable ceremony, though burials were in communal graves, covered with simple boards until full, causing considerable stench. Coffins were sometimes made with a hinged base so that they could be reused after the body was dropped into the grave. The parish bier could be hired to bring the dead to the church,

Right: The ledger stone in St Michael's Church for Revd William and Mrs Ann Marston. (Koll-Art Photography)

Below: The Pauper's Hearse drawn by J. H. Buckingham. (SAMS)

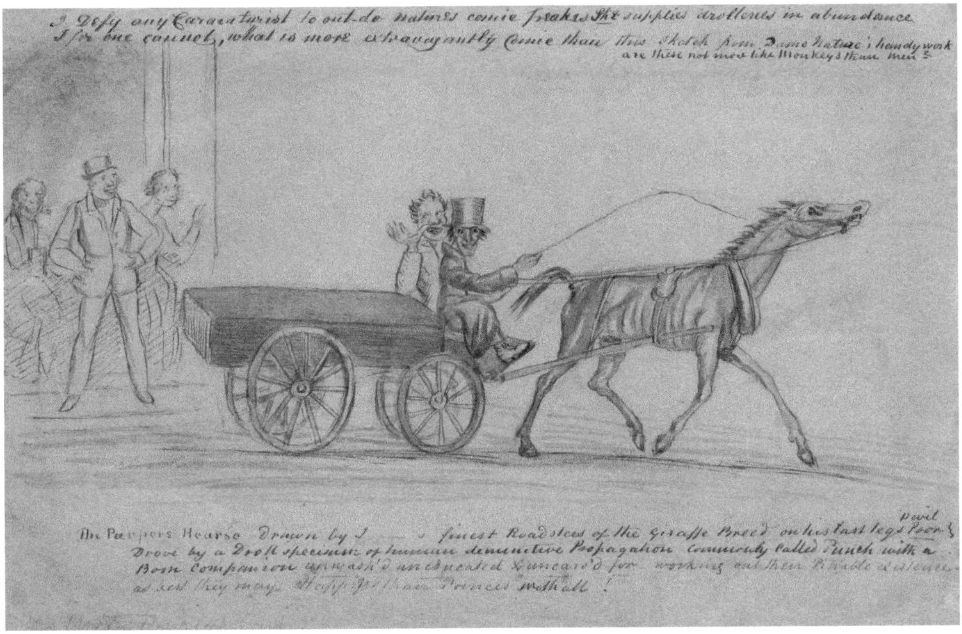

sometimes a long journey – 3 miles from London Colney, or Colney Heath to the church at St Peter's. Small children were often buried in the coffins and graves of other adults. By the late eighteenth century subscription to burial or friendly societies became popular to cover costs as authorities restricted pauper burials to those in the workhouse at the time of death. No one wanted to resort to the workhouse if it could be avoided, especially since, by the mid- nineteenth century, it became legal for the bodies of such paupers to be disposed of to the London anatomy professors.

The ancient practice of burying grave goods with the deceased is long abandoned, though Mrs Lawes (née Bennet) of Rothamsted in Harpenden clearly sought the company of her parents in the hereafter. In a short letter to her son John Bennet Lawes in 1816, the ninety-two-year-old requested that their portraits should be removed from their frames and placed in her coffin on her demise. She too left money for the fine for burial in linen.

Jane Nicholas requested burial in the Abbey Church in St Albans on her death in 1708, despite by then living in Berkhamsted. The trustees' accounts show a payment of three pounds and ten shillings for her coffin and a journey to Berkhamsted, presumably to fetch the corpse. A further two shillings and six pence was paid to the man who went to Berkhamsted to invite mourners to the funeral. The cost of the funeral is not recorded, though she specified 'not more than forty or fifty pounds' should be spent, already a very large sum. The bill for coffin and tomb in the Abbey Church for seventy-four-year-old widow Mrs Elizabeth Lovett, a St Albans butcher, in 1837, was, by contrast, twenty-two pounds. There would then be the standard fees to the minister and sexton, which were doubled for 'out-parishioners'. The tolling of the Great Bell at St Peter's for a funeral cost a further two shillings.

Joseph Handley, whom we have met already, left very explicit directions about his funeral in 1782. It was to take place at midnight, a not uncommon practice which developed in the early seventeenth century. Originally a way of circumventing complicated rules and regulations set by the College of Arms, who were responsible for aristocratic funerals, and determining family successions, it became a status symbol amongst the gentry and upper classes. It demonstrated their ability to pay for the necessary lighting for the funeral procession and burial. In 1764, Mrs Ann Solly of Walthamstow, sister of Mrs Ashurst of St Julian's here, both nonconformists, by contrast requested burial privately by daylight. Handley requested burial in his best suit of clothing and that his lead coffin should be enclosed in another of oak with a brass plate upon it with his name, age and any other pertinent details. A monument was to be erected on the church wall near the family vault similar to that of his brother, but 'handsomer'.

Despite Handley's status in the town, he was not universally respected or liked. A letter from local watchmaker and political agent to John Radcliffe, MP for St Albans, quotes the following:[15]

> Spoken ... by a very old woman in the Abbey workhouse on the death of very wicked man in 1782
>
> If God is pleased when man does cease from sin,
> And Hell is pleased when it a soul doth win,
> And Earth is pleased when it had lost a knave
> Then all is pleased there's Handly [sic] in his Grave.

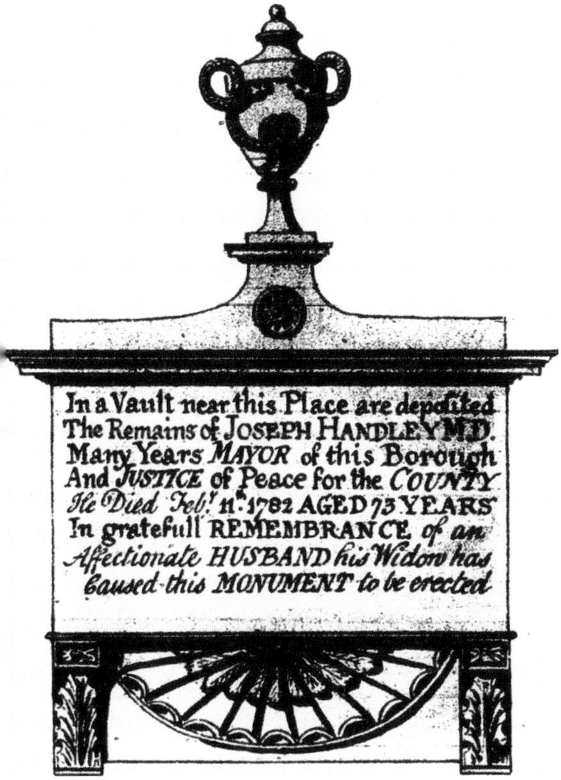

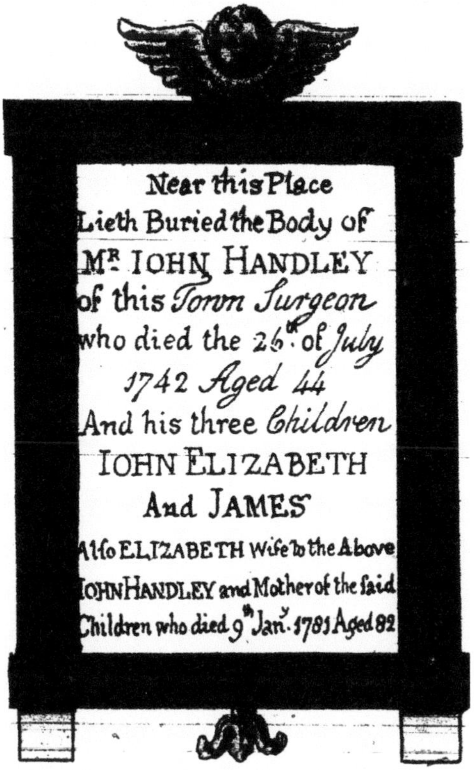

Above left: Original memorial plaque in the Abbey Church for Alderman Dr Joseph Handley, drawn by H. G. Oldfield. (HALS DE/Of/8/147)

Above right: Original memorial plaque in the Abbey Church for surgeon John Handley, drawn by H. G. Oldfield. (HALS DE/Of/8/125)

Resurrection Men

Until the Anatomy Act of 1832 allowed medical men access to the corpses of paupers, they were dependent for their research and teaching on the bodies of executed criminals, or the work of bodysnatchers or 'resurrection men'. Burials in church were fairly secure from such men, but churchyards were much more vulnerable. Graves less than the legal '6 feet under' and unfilled pauper graves were an open invitation. In 1823 the suspicions of two brothers on their way from Harpenden to work at the brickworks on Bernards Heath were aroused by a cart on the road. On arrival, they alerted Mr Fowler, the brickworks manager, who apprehended the men with the cart and found a corpse, later identified as the naked body of William Gillman. The large crowd, which had packed the big courtroom at the subsequent magistrates' hearing, hooted as the men were taken away for trial. The practice of bodysnatching was abhorred, but since bodies, unlike their clothes or shroud, were not the property of anyone, the legalities around stealing them were a grey area. The two men were each given three months in gaol for their misdemeanour. The corpse was held in St Peter's workhouse for reinterment at Luton, where the sexton had thought nothing of the slight disturbance of the grave, having attributed the damage to the cows grazing in the churchyard.

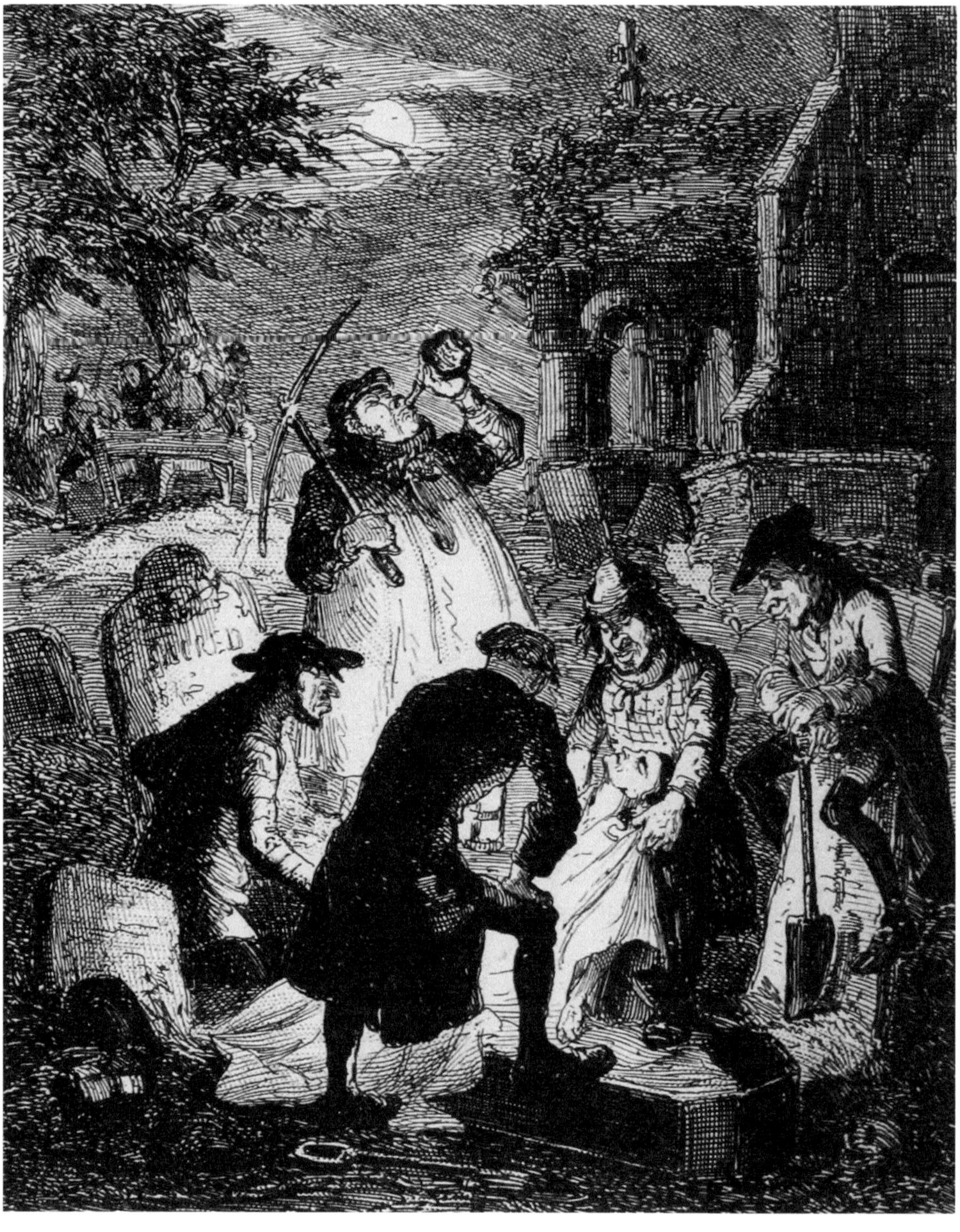

Resurrection men at work drawn by Dickens's illustrator, Hablot Knight Browne ('Phiz') in 1847.

Mourning

Mourning could last a long time and was taken seriously. Wills commonly provided for mourning rings for relatives to ensure the deceased was remembered in perpetuity. Ann Topham wanted twenty people close to her to have rings but said those tenants, other than relatives, invited to her funeral should be given white gloves instead.

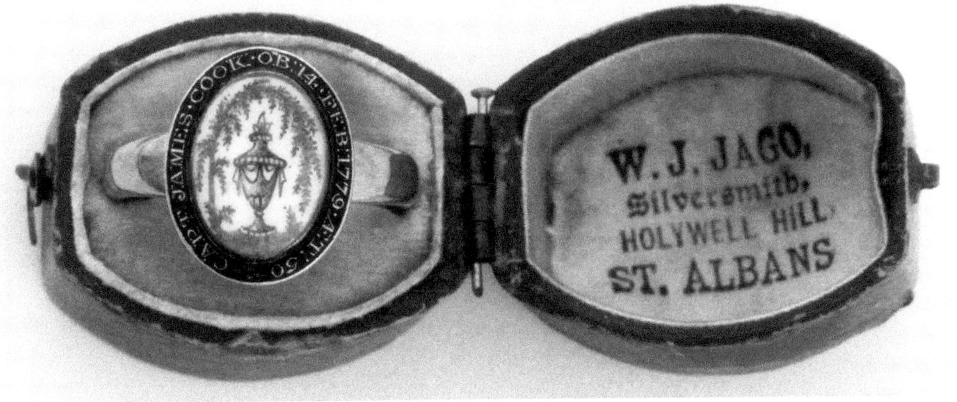

Elizabeth Cook's mourning ring for her husband, Captain James Cook. (NSW State Library)

Captain Cook left no such instructions in the will he wrote as he left on his last fateful voyage in 1776. However, following his death in 1780, his widow, Elizabeth, wore a ring containing a lock of his hair for the rest of her long life. In a box bearing the name and address of jeweller, William Jago, Holywell Hill, St Albans, it is now in the state library of New South Wales. Jago's still trade in St Albans, albeit no longer in the same family or at the same address.

Both widows and widowers frequently remarried, often just one year after bereavement, but usually away from the parish of residence of either party, perhaps as a gesture to decorum.

Wills

Most men with property left a will. Whilst married woman seldom did so, spinsters and widows frequently did. City of London custom entitled a widow to one third of her husband's estate and their children to another third. The final third could be left at the deceased's discretion. This practice was often observed elsewhere too. Where the family fortunes had been dissipated, or where the relevant properties had been leased or mortgaged, a widow might struggle to claim her 'thirds' against the demands of creditors. The widow of Thomas Cox had to resort to litigation for her third of his estate, which included The Vintry on High Street and the Abbey Orchard beyond, since he had many debts.

Another hazard for a widow was the question of 'tail male', whereby the principal family estate passed to the next male in line. In the absence of a son, it could be a more distant relative, who could displace the widow from her home. Elizabeth Ashurst, widowed in 1735 with only a daughter, was obliged to leave their Essex estate at Castle Hedingham, when her husband's brother inherited it. She still had their London home, but rented a country house at St Julian's in St Stephen's as well. To inherit the Gorhambury estate from his great uncle Sir Samuel Grimston in 1700, William Luckyn had to change his name to Grimston.

5. Education and the Town's Schools

The salubrious town, with its fresh air and good water, was attractive to those seeking good educational facilities for their children.

Edward VI's grammar school in the Abbey Church's Lady Chapel drew the young men of respectable families to the town for education as well as providing for local boys. The predecessor of St Albans School, it offered a strictly classical education, though its masters would teach other subjects for a fee. Amongst many notable pupils was John Townshend, later Rear-Admiral and MP, whose mother was niece to the Dowager Countess Spencer. His father sent the precocious lad to the care of Master Revd William Mogg Bowen in 1805 at the age of seven, where, by 1807, he had mastered the classics sufficiently to be made monitor to the other junior classes. He went on in

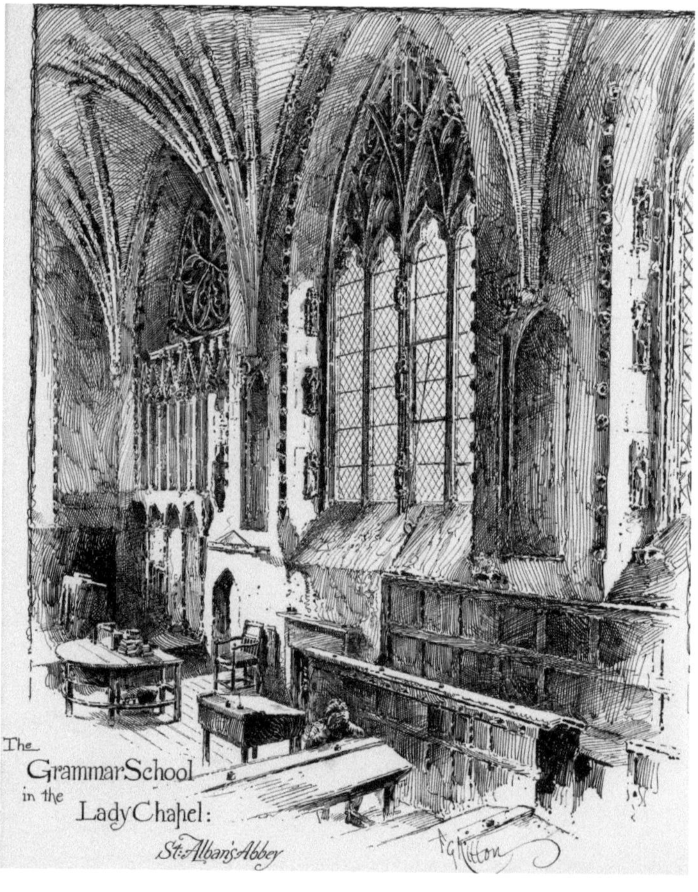

The Grammar School in the Lady Chapel, drawn by F. G. Kitton before it was moved to the Gateway in 1871. (SAMS)

1810 to Eton for two years before joining the Navy. Seventeenth-century alumni include chief justice Sir Francis Pemberton and portrait artist William Dobson, suggested to have been sergeant painter to the king and, according to contemporary John Aubrey, 'the most excellent painter that England has yet bred'. In more recent times, the school has educated Professor Stephen Hawking and Rod Argent of The Zombies.

However, this Establishment-type of education, leading on usually to one of the two universities and the church or the law, was not for all eighteenth-century families. Those in trade, or with broader ideas of education, favoured academies which offered a wider range of subjects such as writing, bookkeeping and surveying. The Dissenting Academies, such as that at Warrington, offered alternative higher education to that of the two universities at Oxford and Cambridge, which required compliance with the Established Church.

Pastor Samuel Clark at the Presbyterian chapel on Dagnall Lane established a charity school for both boys and girls there in 1715. He was mentor there to the orphaned Philip Doddridge, later the noted hymn-writer, and master at the Dissenting Academy in Northampton.

In 1778 teacher, Samuel Heelas, came to St Albans to marry, and opened a school in the house which is now a cosmetic dentist's surgery and the Eurostyle barber's shop opposite St Peter's Church. His St Albans Academy continued until the 1840s, when the classical curriculum at the grammar school was relaxed and pupil numbers there grew.

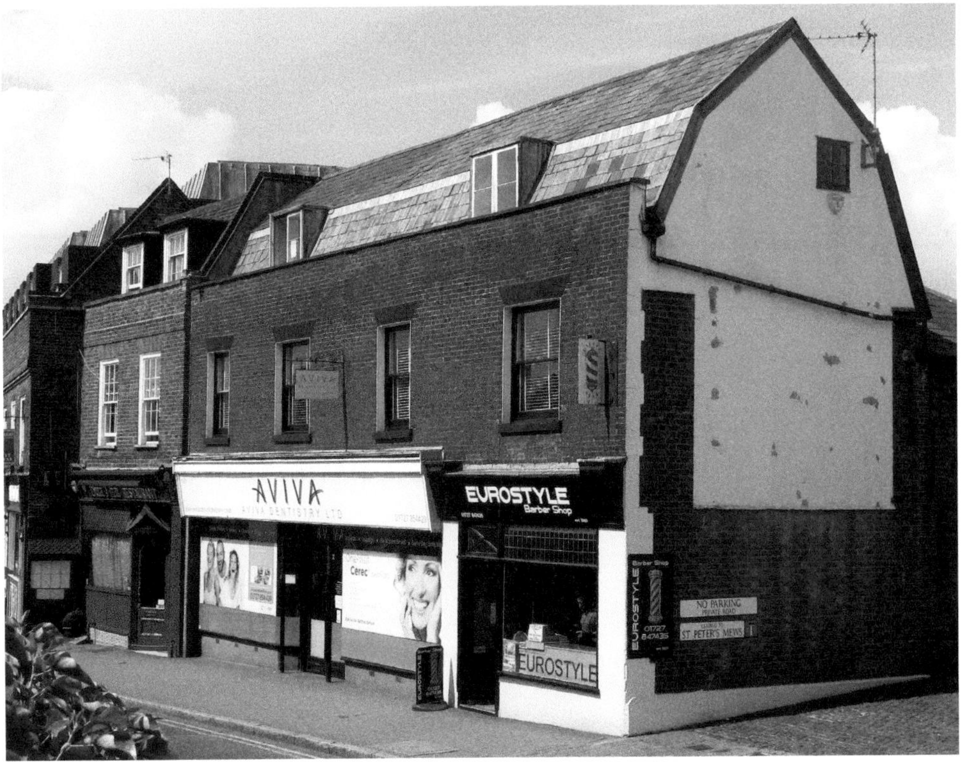

No. 101 St Peter's Street, once the St Albans Academy. (Kari Lundgaard)

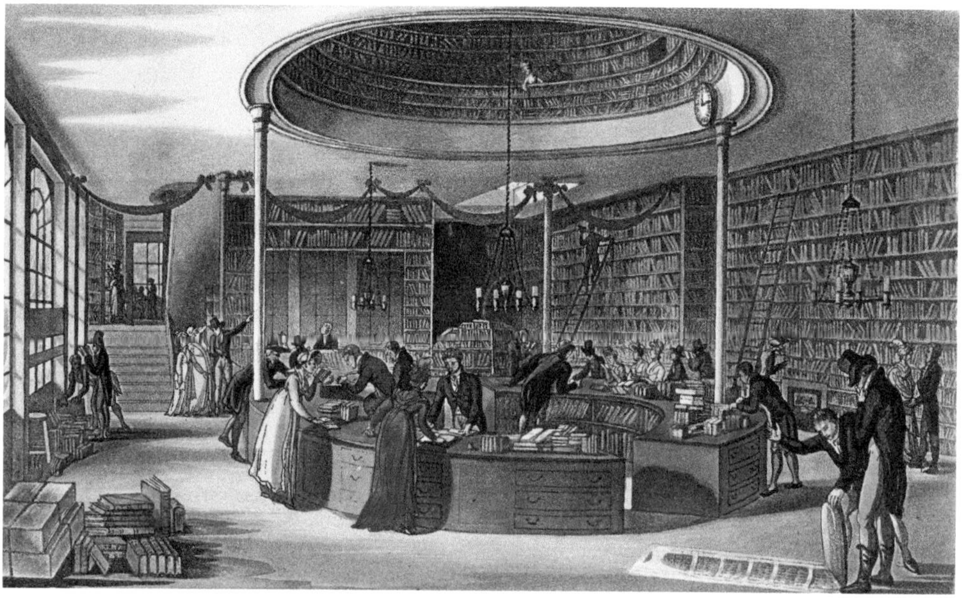

James Lackington's Temple of the Muses.

Heelas and his successors advertised in both London and provincial newspapers and at that fashionable City meeting place, James Lackington's Temple of the Muses. The school accommodated at times around fifty boys.

Boarding school was also a popular option for the daughters of gentry families and St Albans offered more than one of these. The two Misses Wells ran one next door to the academy. One of them later married Baptist minister William Upton, but continued to teach from their London Road home, advertising the 'superior order of both the intellectual and religious advantages and the domestic comforts' offered.

The wife of City merchant Charles Domville, Sarah, daughter of Archdeacon Cole, ran a school for young ladies from The Vintry on High Street. An enquiry from a London lady in 1723 and her response about enrolment was found and reprinted in the *Herts Advertiser* in 1888. Though the daughter of that lady was deemed to be too young for Mrs Domville's school, we learn that dancing was taught for ten shillings entrance and a further ten shillings a quarter, and French the same. Music and dancing were important skills for young ladies and Mrs Domville was probably helped with this by Charles' son, another Charles, later father of Sir William mentioned elsewhere. Charles is recorded as a musician and dancing master and was, from 1750, organist at St Peter's Church.

Schools for the lower echelons of society were offered on Sundays so as not to interfere with the working week of children, especially in farming families. Robert Peel's Act of 1802 required such education to be provided for cotton mill apprentices and a Sunday school was established at the cotton mill in St Albans. Gradually education throughout the week was accepted and National (church) Schools opened in all the St Albans parishes. A British School, in Spencer Street, offered education for those of any, or no, religious persuasion.

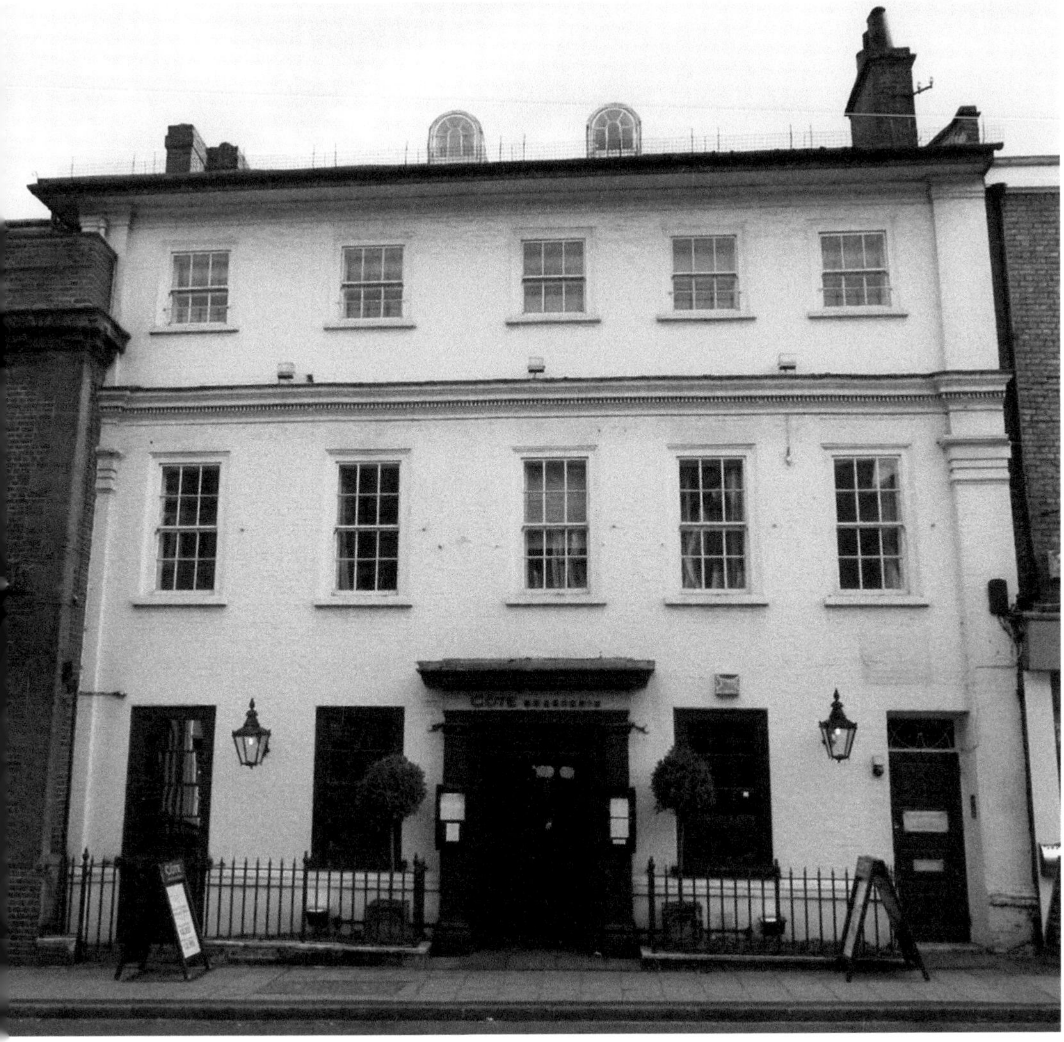

The house that was The Vintry, now Côte restaurant on High Street. (Kari Lundgaard)

DID YOU KNOW?

The celebrated divine Dr Philip Doddridge spent his teenage years in St Albans, educated first at a boarding school in Cock Lane (now Hatfield Road), and then under Dr Samuel Clark, pastor at the Presbyterian chapel in Dagnall Lane from 1711 to 1749.

6. Health and Welfare and the Town's Charities

The distribution of alms to the poor and disadvantaged was a role played by monasteries until their dissolution by Henry VIII. New arrangements had to be made once this huge social upheaval had begun to settle. Under Edward VI, to avoid the need for uncontrolled begging, each parish appointed a collector of contributions from the wealthier members of the community to provide alms for the poor. This soon proved to be totally insufficient,

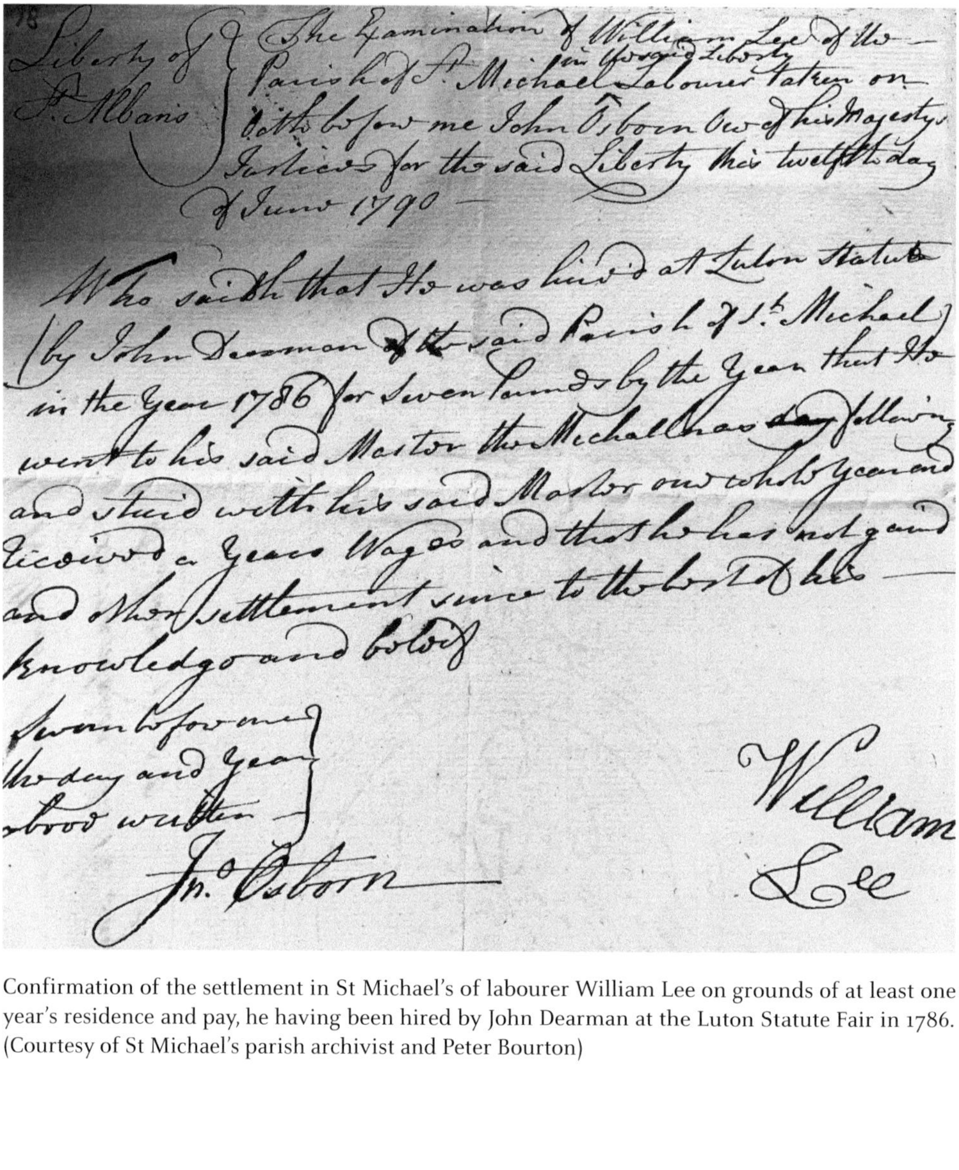

Liberty of St. Albans } The Examination of William Lee of the Parish of St. Michael in the foresaid Liberty Labourer taken on Oath before me John Osborn One of his Majesty's Justices for the said Liberty this twelfth day of June 1790 —

Who saith that He was hired at Luton Statute (by John Dearman of the said Parish of St. Michael) in the Year 1786 for Seven Pounds by the Year that He went to his said Master the Michaelmas ~~day~~ following and staid with his said Master one whole Year and Received a Years Wages and that he has not gained any other Settlement since to the best of his Knowledge and belief

Sworn before me the day and Year above written

Jno. Osborn

William Lee

Confirmation of the settlement in St Michael's of labourer William Lee on grounds of at least one year's residence and pay, he having been hired by John Dearman at the Luton Statute Fair in 1786. (Courtesy of St Michael's parish archivist and Peter Bourton)

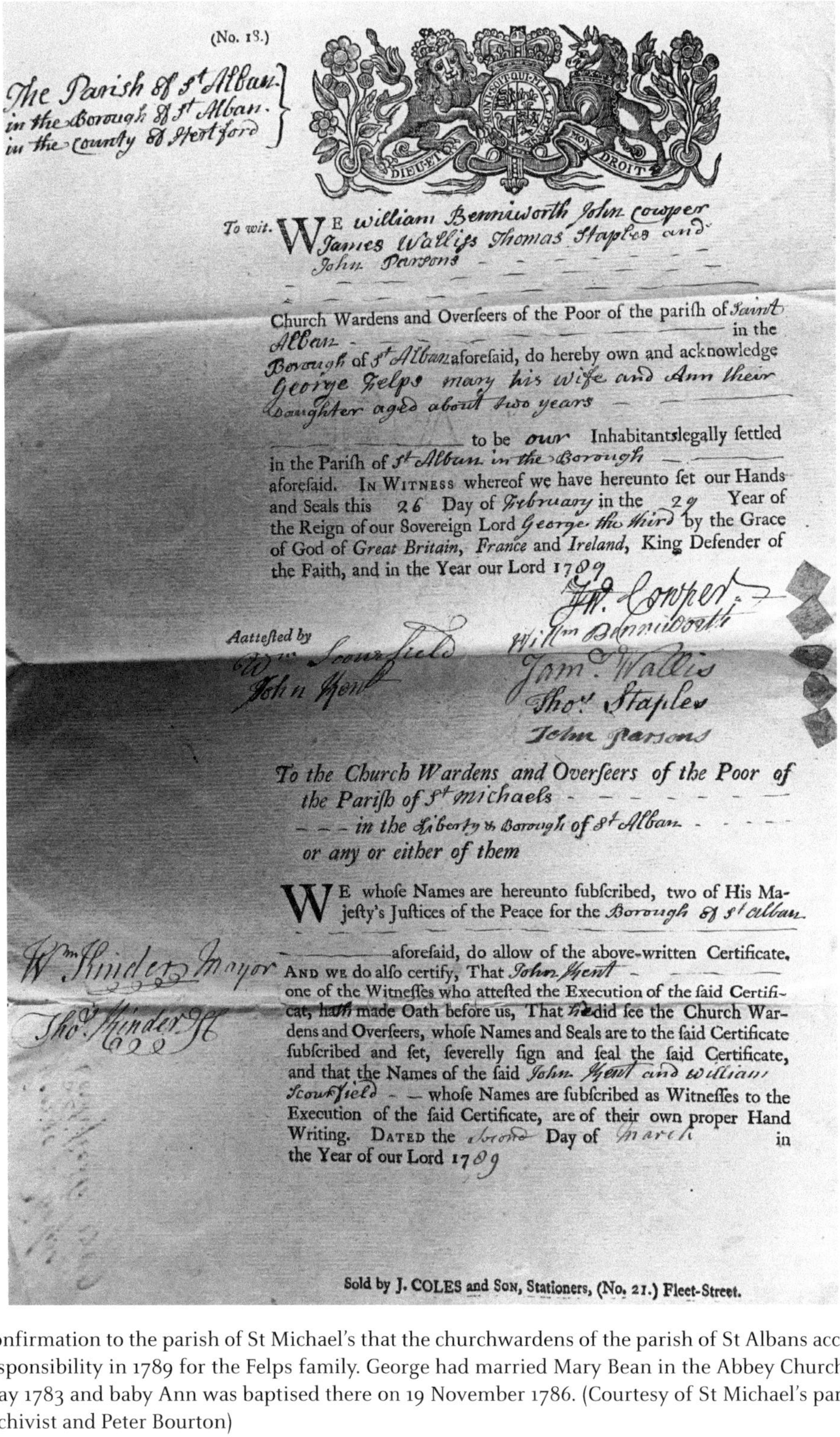

(No. 18.)

The Pariſh of St Alban in the Borough of St Alban in the County of Hertford

To wit. WE William Benniworth John Cowper James Wallis Thomas Staples and John Parsons

Church Wardens and Overſeers of the Poor of the pariſh of Saint Alban in the Borough of St Alban aforeſaid, do hereby own and acknowledge George Felps Mary his wife and Ann their Daughter aged about two years to be our Inhabitants legally ſettled in the Pariſh of St Alban in the Borough aforeſaid. In Witness whereof we have hereunto ſet our Hands and Seals this 26 Day of February in the 29 Year of the Reign of our Sovereign Lord George the third by the Grace of God of *Great Britain*, *France* and *Ireland*, King Defender of the Faith, and in the Year our Lord 1789

Jn. Cowper
Willm Benniworth
Jam. Wallis
Thos Staples
John Parsons

Aatteſted by
Wm Scourfield
John Kent

To the Church Wardens and Overſeers of the Poor of the Pariſh of St Michaels in the Liberty & Borough of St Alban or any or either of them

WE whoſe Names are hereunto ſubſcribed, two of His Majeſty's Juſtices of the Peace for the Borough of St Alban aforeſaid, do allow of the above-written Certificate. And we do alſo certify, That John Kent one of the Witneſſes who atteſted the Execution of the ſaid Certificat, hath made Oath before us, That he did ſee the Church Wardens and Overſeers, whoſe Names and Seals are to the ſaid Certificate ſubſcribed and ſet, ſeverelly ſign and ſeal the ſaid Certificate, and that the Names of the ſaid John Kent and William Scoufield whoſe Names are ſubſcribed as Witneſſes to the Execution of the ſaid Certificate, are of their own proper Hand Writing. Dated the second Day of March in the Year of our Lord 1789

Wm Kinder Mayor
Thos Kinder

Sold by J. COLES and Son, Stationers, (No. 21.) Fleet-Street.

Confirmation to the parish of St Michael's that the churchwardens of the parish of St Albans accept responsibility in 1789 for the Felps family. George had married Mary Bean in the Abbey Church in May 1783 and baby Ann was baptised there on 19 November 1786. (Courtesy of St Michael's parish archivist and Peter Bourton)

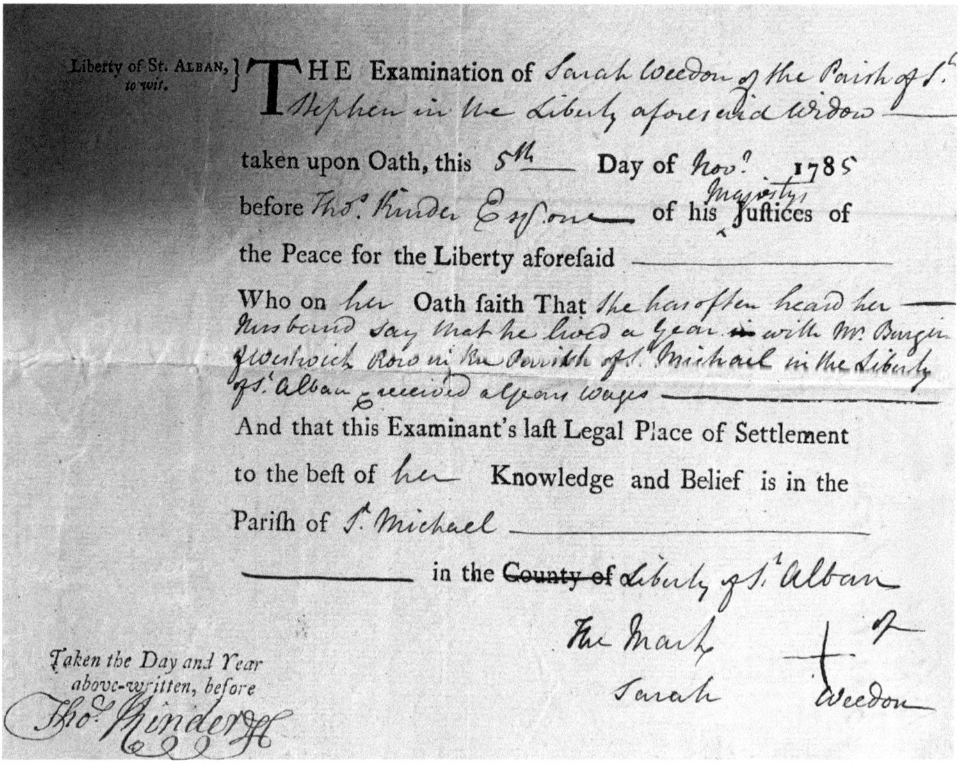

Liberty of St. ALBAN, to wit. } THE Examination of Sarah Weedon of the Parish of St. Stephen in the Liberty aforesaid Widow

taken upon Oath, this 5th Day of Nov.r 1785

before Thos. Kinder Esq. one of his Majesty's Justices of the Peace for the Liberty aforesaid

Who on her Oath saith That she has often heard her Husband say that he lived a Year with Mr. Burgin of Westwick Row in the Parish of St. Michael in the Liberty of St. Alban & received a years Wages

And that this Examinant's last Legal Place of Settlement to the best of her Knowledge and Belief is in the Parish of St. Michael

in the ~~County of~~ Liberty of St. Alban

The Mark + of Sarah Weedon

Taken the Day and Year above-written, before Thos. Kinder

Widow Sarah Weedon claimed settlement in St Michael's on grounds of her husband having established settlement there. (Courtesy of St Michael's parish archivist and Peter Bourton)

and legislation followed which required each parish to ensure a certain standard of living for all. 'Correction' ensured the poor made an effort on their own behalf, but the disadvantaged could expect parish support. The poor rate provided 'outdoor relief' or financial support, or sometimes clothing and shoes. Orphaned children were placed with parish families until they could be put out as apprentices. The parish paid the apprentices' premium, but they were bound for longer than the standard seven years, often until they were twenty-five years old.

The entitlement to support was limited to those who could prove 'settlement'. Claims of those who had recently moved into a parish would not be supported. They would be returned to their most recent parish of settlement. A settlement certificate – an early passport – was issued on the basis of residence in a parish without complaint for more than forty days, a contract for employment there for more than a year and a day, or for a seven-year apprenticeship, rent from a property worth more than ten pounds, or having been born or married there.

Return to parish of settlement could involve a short trip up the road, as for Elizabeth Dolloway in May 1691, who was returned from the Abbey parish to St Peter's,[16] or a long trip in a cart over one parish boundary after another to a different part of the country. For all of this, parish boundaries had to be clear, sometimes with physical marking,

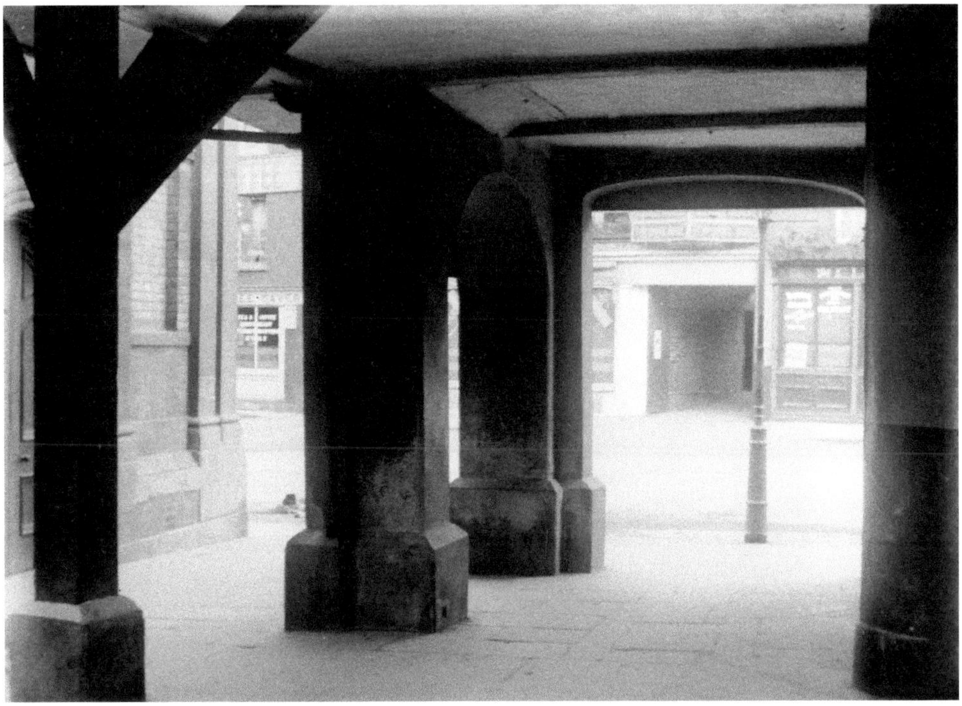

Above: The beams in Lamb Alley near the Market Place with a mark indicating the boundary between St Peter's and the Abbey parish. (SAHAAS)

Right: Warrant issued in 1780 by Joseph Handley, mayor of St Albans, for the arrest of Thomas Lawrence, he having fathered a child with Sara Roft, who would become a charge of St Michael's parish. (Courtesy of St Michael's parish archivist and Peter Bourton)

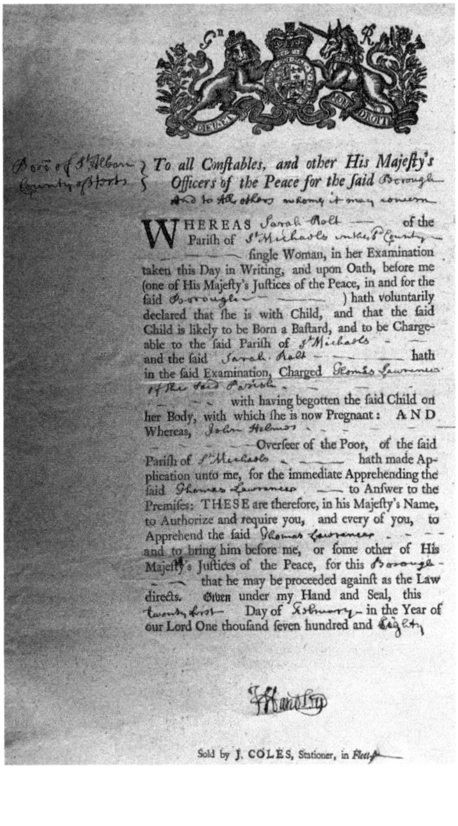

Boro of St Albans County of Herts } *To all Conſtables, and other His Majeſty's Officers of the Peace for the ſaid* Borough And to all others whom it may concern

WHEREAS Sarah Rolt — of the Pariſh of St Michaels in the sd County — ſingle Woman, in her Examination taken this Day in Writing, and upon Oath, before me (one of His Majeſty's Juſtices of the Peace, in and for the ſaid Borough —) hath voluntarily declared that ſhe is with Child, and that the ſaid Child is likely to be Born a Baſtard, and to be Chargeable to the ſaid Pariſh of St Michaels — and the ſaid Sarah Rolt — hath in the ſaid Examination, Charged Thomas Lawrence of the said Parish — with having begotten the ſaid Child on her Body, with which ſhe is now Pregnant: AND Whereas, John Holmes — Overſeer of the Poor, of the ſaid Pariſh of St Michaels — hath made Application unto me, for the immediate Apprehending the ſaid Thomas Lawrence — to Anſwer to the Premiſes: THESE are therefore, in his Majeſty's Name, to Authorize and require you, and every of you, to Apprehend the ſaid Thomas Lawrence — and to bring him before me, or ſome other of His Majeſty's Juſtices of the Peace, for this Borough — that he may be proceeded againſt as the Law directs. Given under my Hand and Seal, this twenty first Day of February in the Year of our Lord One thouſand ſeven hundred and Eighty

Sold by J. COLES, Stationer, in Fleet-st

such as in Lamb Alley in the Market Place between the Abbey parish and St Peter's, but often endorsed by ceremonial 'beating' of the bounds.

For the avoidance of a potential claim, in 1733, St Peter's parish Vestry made an Order binding young Thomas Cox, son of Thomas of The Vintry, and indeed his elder brother, in the sum of fifty pounds to pay for the maintenance and education of the child Thomas had allegedly fathered with Mary Brownsell. Both boys were still in apprenticeships, so could not marry, and Thomas was under twenty-one, the age of maturity until 1970. By then orphaned and still a minor, Thomas's brother had to stand surety for him. With that family's financial problems, St Peter's churchwardens were taking no chances.

The father of Sarah Roft's child had clearly already absconded and was being pursued by the authorities in her parish.

The deserving poor were treated sympathetically, with either free or low rent accommodation in parish or charity properties. The Pemberton Almshouses, on St Peter's Street, built in brick in 1634 for six poor widows, still offer such housing, but from the District Council; others are still run by charitable trusts.

Workhouses

The ever-increasing burden of supporting the poor led to the establishment in the early eighteenth century of houses where paupers could live and work. Each of the St Albans parishes had workhouses. St Stephen's, just outside the borough, was on Watling Street

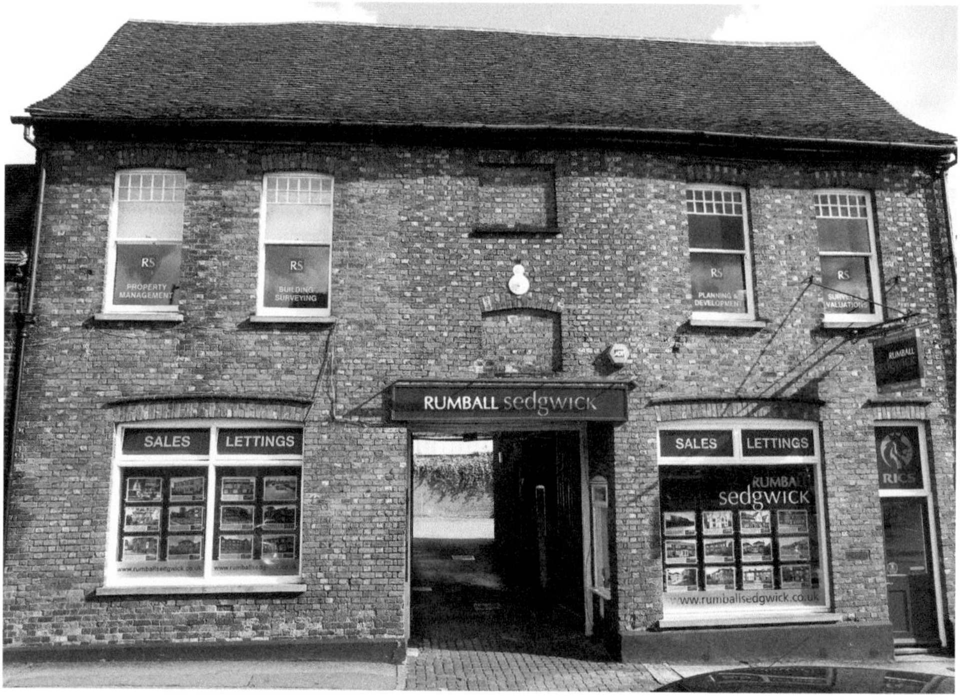

St Peter's parish workhouse, now the offices of Rumball Sedgwick, chartered surveyors. (Kari Lundgaard)

opposite the church, and is now a private house. St Peter's is the offices of Rumball, Sedgwick, estate agents. St Stephen's could accommodate 100 persons. In 1723 twenty of the older men and women there were winding cotton wicks for tallow chandlers' candles, whilst ten boys made horse whips and four girls were spinning linen and wool. All the workhouses had a nursery garden, which at St Stephen's was an acre and a half, some of which was let to a gardener. St Peter's inventory of 1757 listed spinning wheels, and a spade, a fork and a weedhook, no doubt for garden work. Inmates provided their own bedding.

A medical officer was paid a fixed salary for care of the poor. Through much of the eighteenth century, both St Michael's and St Peter's parishes paid surgeon and man-midwife Joseph Handley ten pounds a year. The son of a retired naval surgeon, Handley held many roles and responsibilities in the town. In 1757 he obtained a medical degree from the University of Aberdeen, though seems never to have attended there. He then assumed the title Doctor, having found three friendly colleagues to nominate him to the College of Physicians.

Charities

Besides providing almshouses and workhouses, parish officers administered legacies left for the benefit of the parish and its poor. This could be for an annual sermon, the fabric of the church, education or clothing for the poor or even regular distribution of bread. Such legacies ensured a smooth passage to heaven and a clear conscience for the benefactor, though by the eighteenth century were simply charitable acts. A mid-nineteenth century survey suggested that more than 400 people in the town were benefitted in this way. Many small bequests have been lost or amalgamated over time, though several survive today, such as the Jane Nicholas Charity and Kentish's Educational Foundation, established in 1708 and 1712, respectively.

The Jane Nicholas Charity and John Dunton

Wealthy widow Jane Nicholas left her entire estate in trust for the elderly poor of the St Albans parishes, effectively cutting out her one surviving daughter, Sarah, and the wayward husband, London publisher John Dunton, whom she had, in 1697, married at St Peter's Church.

John Dunton was a flamboyant character more than ten years older than his bride. He founded the Athenian Society and its eponymous journal, whose four members had included his brother-in-law Revd Samuel Wesley, father of John, Charles and Samuel Jr. In this successful journal he provided an agony aunt column. Dunton and/or Wesley answered questions on 'divinity, history, philosophy, mathematics, love, poetry'. They soon also received questions from ladies and this led to the publication for a brief four weeks in 1693 of the *Ladies' Mercury*, in which Dunton answered 'all the most nice and curious questions concerning love, marriage, behaviour, dress and humour of the female sex, whether virgins, wives, or widows'. Crisis had come for Dunton when Wesley obtained a living at Epworth and so moved to Lincolnshire and then his wife, Elizabeth (neé Annesley), to whom he was devoted, died. Dunton's life fell apart and he was in a state of financial crisis too.

Dunton's marriage to Sarah Nicholas must have been some kind of saving grace. However, his flamboyant lifestyle and speculative ventures were to cause friction, especially with his new mother-in-law. The couple separated, more than once, but finally following both Sarah and her mother's refusal to pay Dunton's increasing debts. Dunton wrote to a friend, complaining of the situation whilst protesting his love for the wife he called his Valeria and respect for her mother. The friend showed his case to Sarah, prompting this reply of 1701, the original of which is held in the Bodleian Library:

> I write to let you know, that if you think of providing for me, I am very willing you should have all your *yoke and burden,* as you call it being married, removed, and return me my fortune and we will be both single; and you shall have your land if you will return me my money, and sure that will please you; for I, and all good people, think you never married me for love but for my money; and so you have had the use of it all this while to banter and laugh at me and my mother by your maggoty Printers

In recognition of his wayward lifestyle, in 1705 Dunton wrote *The Life and Errors of John Dunton ... with an Idea of a New Life.* However, this was not enough to pre-empt Jane Nicholas' decision to exclude him from her will, though she left Sarah a life interest in the estate. Extraordinarily, she also requested that her charitable legacies should be engraved on her tomb in the Abbey Church, though this seems not to have been done.

Dunton challenged the will, and, with Sarah, made an agreement with the trustees for a quarterly payment of sixty pounds each during their lifetimes, with the residue of the income to Sarah for life – but this did not materialise. Dunton and Sarah took the trustees to court, but in vain. Dunton received nothing, the couple were never reconciled, and Sarah died alone in 1721. At that point, Dunton gave it one more try, but the trustees were obdurate. He obtained nothing. Seven years later, still smarting from his treatment by his mother-in-law, he wrote an *Essay on Deathbed Charity,* in which he showed that large bequests to the poor are no charity at all, but a sort of compounding with God Almighty for miserliness in lifetime. He referred not only to Jane Nicholas, but also to Thomas Guy, a fellow bookseller. He understood Guy to have underpaid his employees, but then left money to found the eponymous Guy's Hospital in London. His great wealth came, in fact, from his successful speculation with the South Sea Company rather more than from any sharp business practice in bookselling.

The poor, then, relied on charities, such as that of Jane Nicholas, but with successive trustees legitimately claiming salaries and lawyers charging for administration, the moneys available were often eroded. In 1822 the Jane Nicholas Charity was found to have been embezzled by one of its trustees, and aldermen in the town obliged by the Court of Chancery to return funds they had 'borrowed' from such charitable funds under their control. Such was the vulnerability of provision for the poor, despite donors' best intentions, until the twentieth century introduction of the welfare state.

The Introduction of the Unions

Individual parishes were relieved of their responsibility for the poor with the reforms of the 1830s and the formation of Unions. An elected Board of Guardians set up the

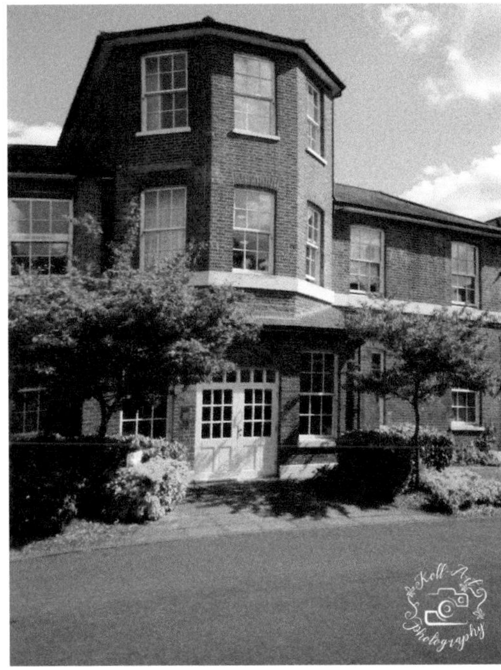

Right: The Union workhouse on the St Albans City Hospital site, now apartments. (Koll-Art Photography)

Below: The Workhouse Treat on the King Harry meadow. J. H. Buckingham. (SAMS)

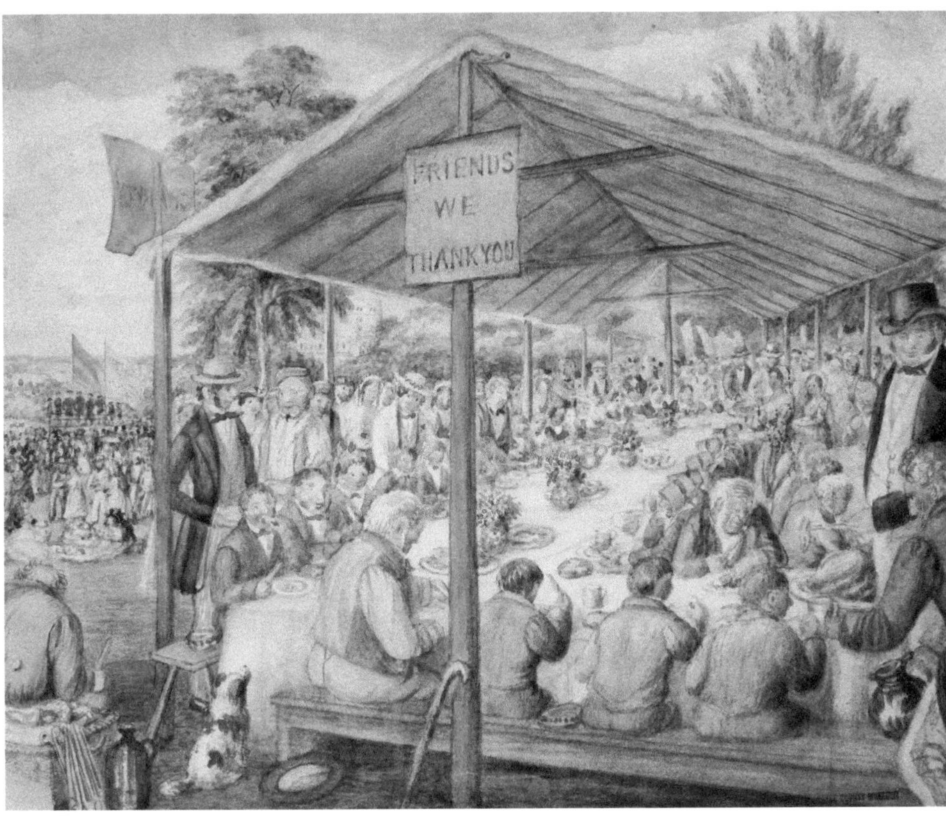

St Albans Union for six adjacent parishes in 1838 and built a new workhouse on the present City Hospital site. This was a huge establishment which operated until well into the twentieth century. Satirist J. H. Buckingham's drawing of the Workhouse Treat shows the irony of the patronage which was bestowed on the unfortunate in the mid-nineteenth century. The building is now smart apartments.

Hospitals

Most parishes provided a pest house for isolation and care. St Albans had one; that of St Stephen's parish was in Park Street and still so named into the nineteenth century. Surgeons provided the service of bleeding and primitive surgical treatment, whilst apothecaries dispensed medicines and herbal remedies. Their training was by apprenticeship. Physicians were university trained and titled Doctor, but could offer only limited advice with a bedside manner. Diagnosis was limited, and consultations were often by correspondence.

In 1844 a dispensary was opened in St Albans in rented rooms on Holywell Hill. It was open on Tuesday and Saturday mornings from nine until eleven. Run by committee, a dispenser, for many years the pharmacist and chemist Henry Gilham Martin was paid ten pounds a year. He was later proprietor of St Albans Holywell Mineral Waters and a mayor of the borough.

In 1861 a site on the East side of the hill, next to the Crown Inn on the corner of Sopwell Lane, where Abbey Court flats now stand, was acquired for a purpose-built hospital to accommodate in-patients. The two-storey hospital, designed by Sir George Gilbert Scott 'in quiet Gothic style' and paid for by subscriptions, was opened in 1871.

Principal subscriber was Mrs Isabella Worley of New Barnes, now run as Sopwell House Hotel. Medical man and noted antiquarian Ridgway Lloyd, who had recently bought a practice in the town, offered his services gratis. After seventeen years' service,

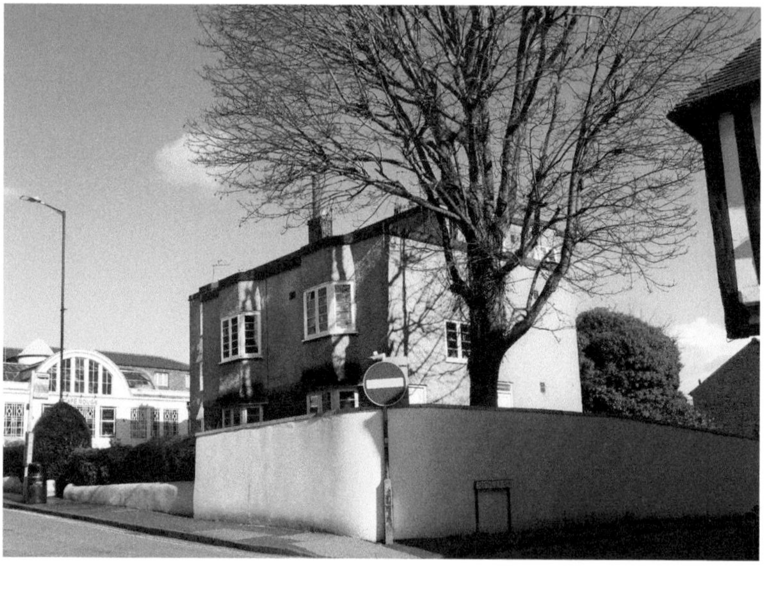

Abbey Court flats on Holywell Hill – the site of the first purpose-built hospital in St Albans. (Kari Lundgaard)

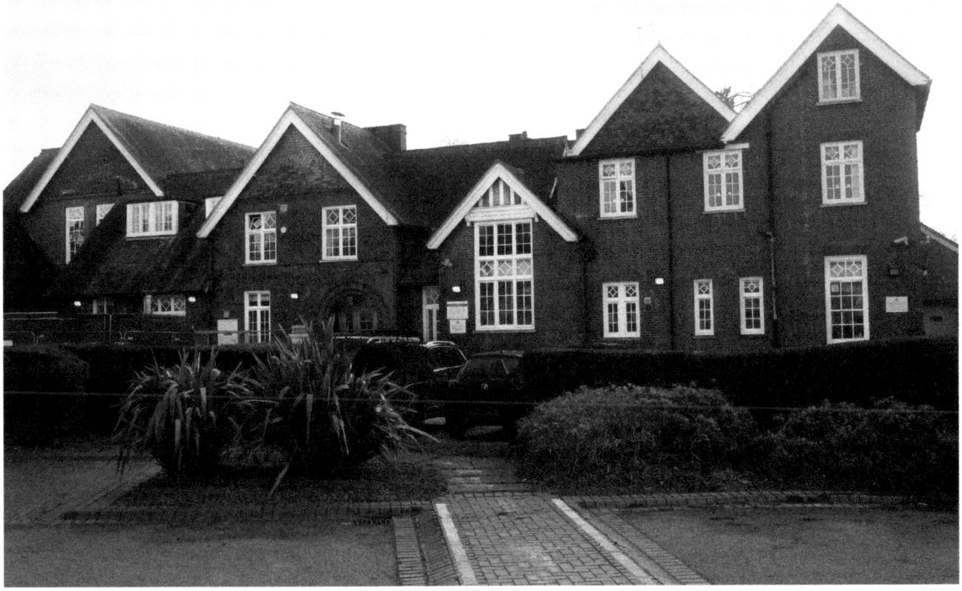

The hospital on Verulam Road, opened in 1888, now occupied partly by the Muriel Green Nursery. (Kari Lundgaard)

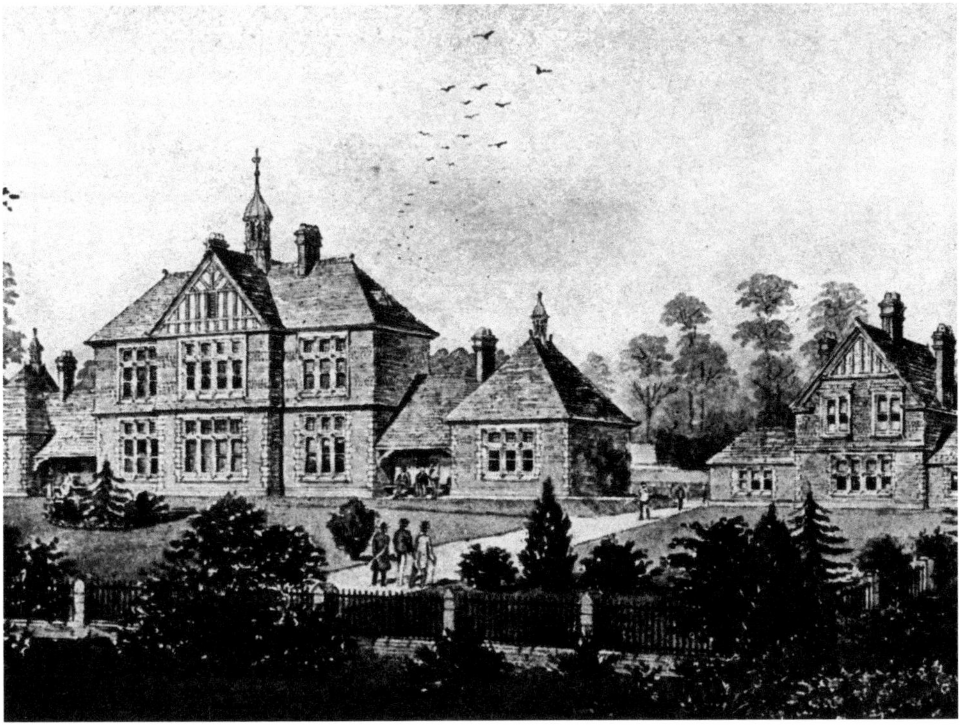

Sir John Blundell Maple's Sisters' Hospital. (SAMS)

larger premises were taken on the corner of Verulam Road and Church Crescent, and a new hospital opened by the Earl of Verulam on 10 October 1888 with the mayor and Corporation attending in state. The redundant Holywell Hill building was used by the newly established High School for Girls until their move to Townsend Avenue in 1908.

The Mid Herts Hospital on Verulam Road, much extended over the years, finally amalgamated with the institutions at Oster Hills, the former Union Workhouse, the Sisters' Hospital for Infectious Diseases and Oster House to form St Albans City Hospital. The Sisters' Hospital had been built, equipped and furnished by Sir John Blundell Maple in 1893, for the free treatment of all patients in the town. His two daughters, Winifred and Dorothy, had both died of scarlet fever.

Mental Health

In the 1830s and '40s there had been a lunatic asylum at Oster House run by James Quilter Rumball, brother of the surveyor and estate agent John Horner Rumball. James Quilter had assisted their father, another doctor, who had run a similar institution earlier at The Holt on Watford Road. James Quilter was an advocate of phrenology, touring widely giving lectures on the subject.

As early as 1757 there had also been a mental health institution in St Albans. Dr Nathaniel Cotton rented the College, a large estate on Dagnall Lane, for just that purpose. He called it his Collegium Insanorum. Well regarded for the humane care he

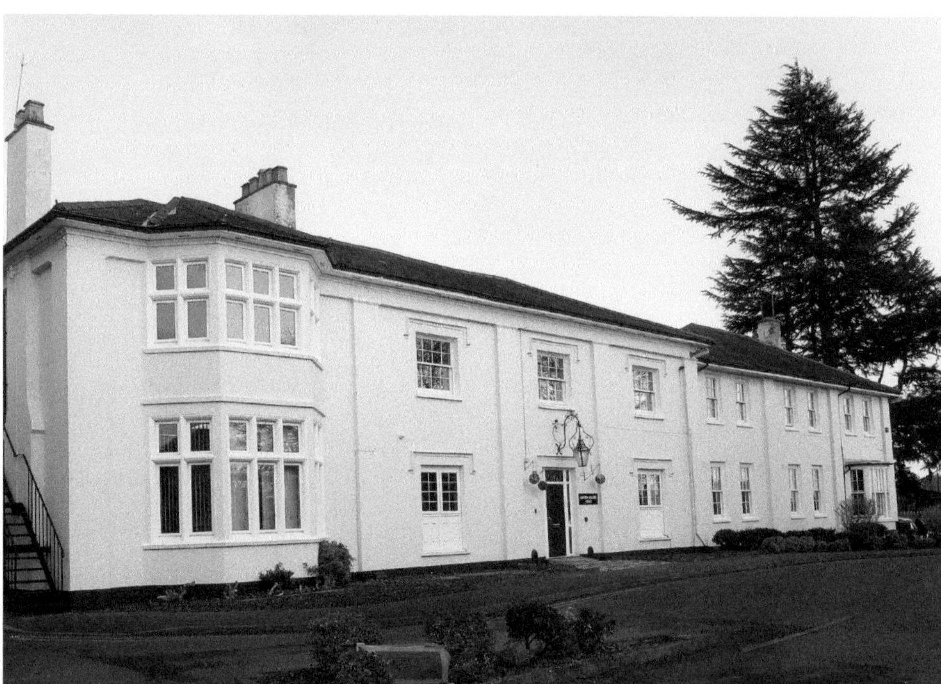

Oster House, built as a gentleman's residence in 1827, and now providing sheltered accommodation. (Kari Lundgaard)

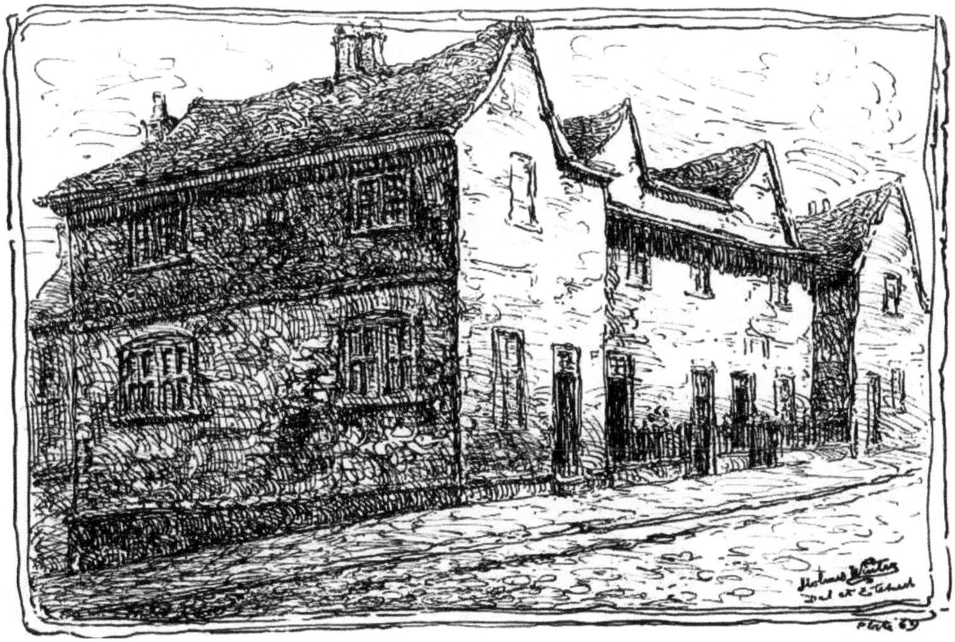

Above: The College, drawn in 1898 by Holmes Winter. (SAMS)

Right: Posthumous drawing of the poet William Cowper who spent time at The College from 1763. (SAMS)

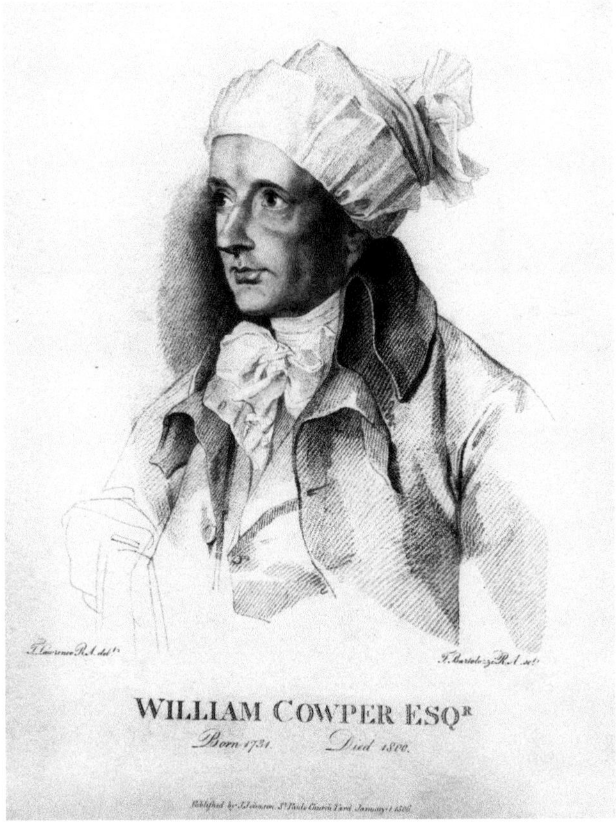

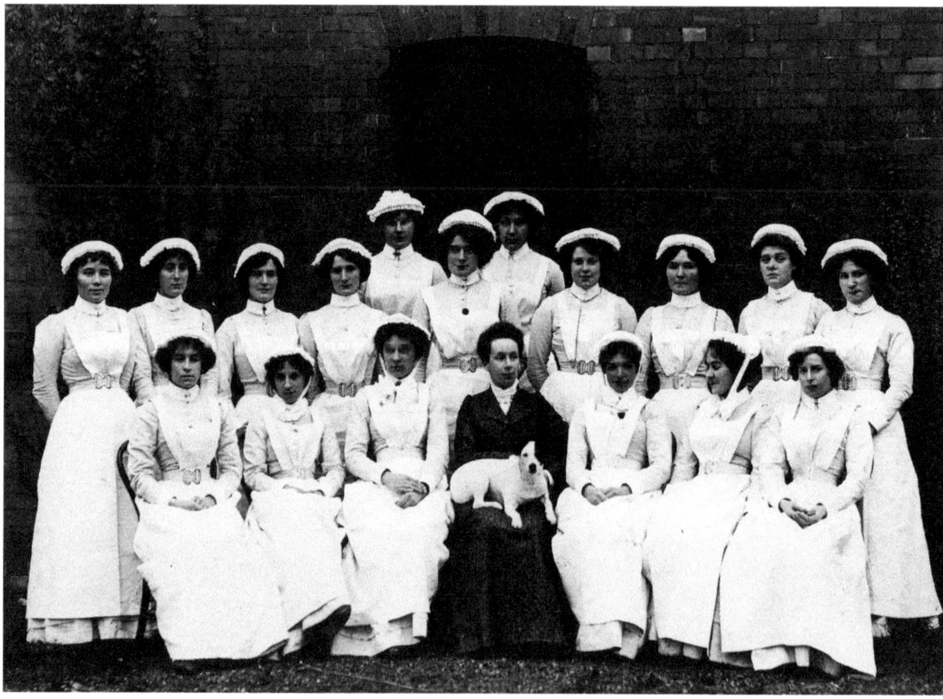

Nurses at Hill End Hospital in 1904 by local photographer A. Montiville-Evans. (SAMS)

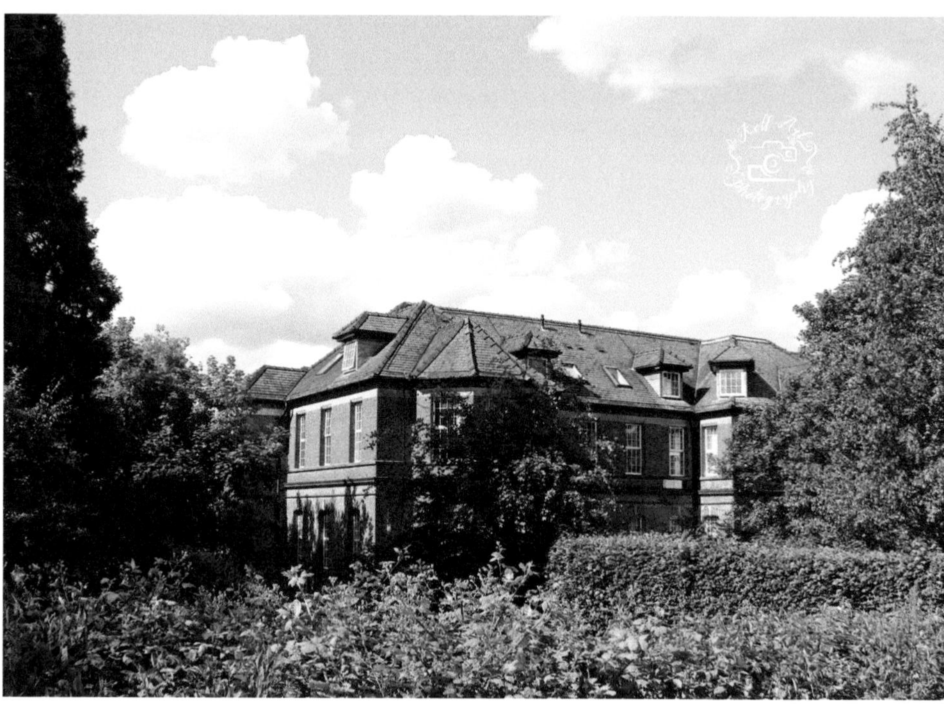

Hill End Hospital, now apartments. (Koll-Art Photography)

gave his patients, it was for two years home to the poet William Cowper, who wrote favourably about his time there.

These were commercial establishments, though such places were subject to inspection by the authorities. By the late nineteenth century, it was thought preferable for such patients to be cared for in the wide-open spaces and fresh air of the countryside, and hospitals were built on estates outside London to accommodate them. Six such establishments were opened in Hertfordshire south of St Albans.

Hill End Hospital, which could accommodate over 1,000 patients, was opened in 1899 specifically for the mentally ill of Hertfordshire.

It was a prime estate of nearly 600 acres close to the Hatfield to St Albans railway line and almost self-sufficient with the patients helping on the farm and looking after the livestock. The hospital finally closed in 1995, with the late twentieth-century change in philosophy to favour care in the community over the institutionalisation which had resulted from these purpose-built establishments. They have all now been redeveloped to meet the ever-pressing housing needs of the South East.

7. Support for the Deserving Poor – The Patronage of the Dowager Countess Spencer

Agricultural and other workers in and around St Albans were badly affected by the prevailing poor harvests, deprivations of wartime and the high prices of essential foodstuffs of the late eighteenth century, with many looking to the parish for welfare. Frederick Morton Eden's survey of the labouring poor following the grain crises of 1794/5 showed that the poor rate assessment in St Albans had almost doubled between 1776 and 1786, but also that the opening of workhouses in the 1720s had at that time reduced the rate required over the following decade.

On the death of the 1st Earl Spencer in 1783, his widow, Georgiana (née Poyntz), had chosen Holywell House, at the foot of Holywell Hill, as her new home. Maintaining the family's interest at election times became her principal role, though her natural philanthropy also led her to many social activities in the town, much to do with women and education.

She ran the apartments of her forebear, the Duchess of Marlborough, known as The Buildings, personally, usually placing single or widowed women she knew there, and then visiting regularly.

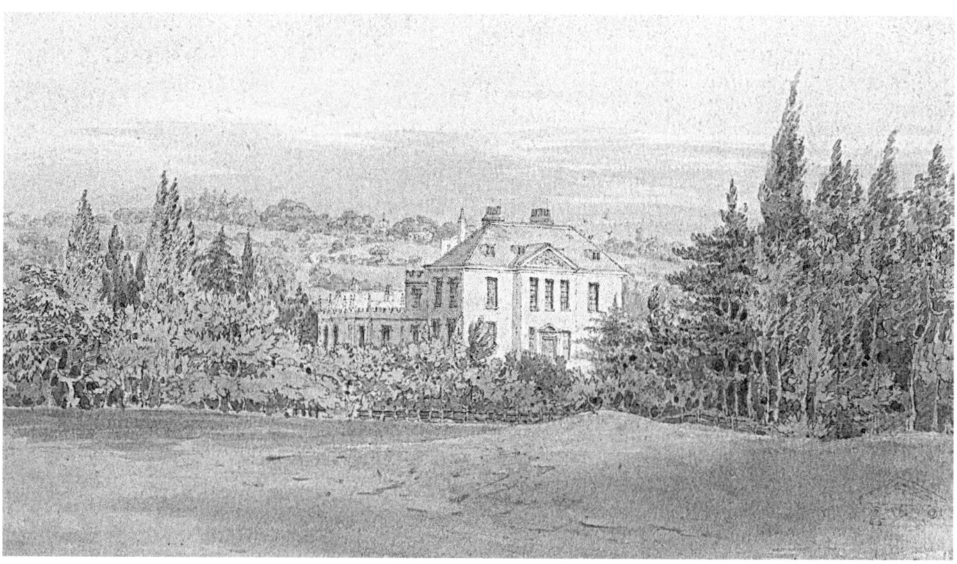

Watercolour wash over a pencil drawing of Holywell House. (SAMS)

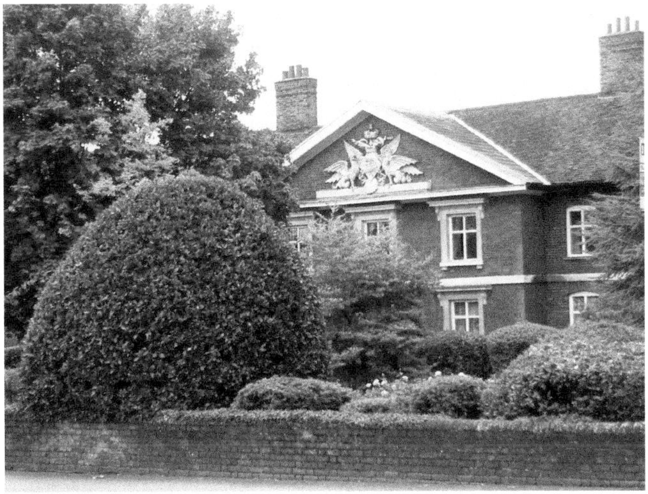

The Buildings, which replaced the manor house of Newland Squillers, on Cock Lane, in 1733. (Kari Lundgaard)

She founded both a Sunday school, and an Industrial School for Girls which provided clothing and prepared the girls for service in gentry households.

St Albans School of Industry Expenditure for 12 Girls in 1791
£17.9.2¼d

- 12 camlet gowns
- 12 checked bibs and aprons
- 24 caps, bindes and tippits
- Worsted for 12 pr of stockings
- 12 straw hats and trimming
- 12 yards of tape
- 6 pair of stays
- Needles, forms and pegs
- 4 spinning wheels & carriage
- 3 doz of flax
- knitting needles
- tow and beeswax
- a lock and key for a box
- 12 workbags
- 3/6 to Waller and Sage* for attending the subscribers' meeting
- 1 school book 1/8
- 35 weeks schooling £6.5.0.

*Sage was a waggoner in Holywell Ward

The Countess called on gentry colleagues to support her by subscribing to these institutions. The Hon Mrs Walter, mother-in-law to Viscount Grimston, Mrs Keller, Mrs Spooner, Mrs and the Miss Domville, all subscribed for the Industrial School, whose pupils they would later employ in their households, typically contributing one or two guineas each. Since no teacher is mentioned in the records it is possible the Countess taught the girls herself.

DID YOU KNOW?

St Albans had a Friendly Society exclusively for women. The St Albans Female Friendly Society was founded in 1801 by the Dowager Countess Spencer, who lived at Holywell House. It had more than 100 members, who all contributed three pence a week towards their lying-in, pensions and funeral expenses. If sick and unable to work, they received a small allowance. Wealthy ladies in the town subscribed to support the society.

Self-help Organisations and Benefactors

Whilst many of the better-off members of society throughout the country supported their poor, they also encouraged self-help, in the interests of minimising the burden on the rates their parishes levied.

Sir Thomas Bernard's Society for Bettering the Condition and Increasing the Comforts of the Poor, founded in 1796, sought not only to provide relief, but to educate and give support in good and moral living and self-reliance. The society collected and reported examples of good practice around the country.

Rice and Beef for the Poor

No doubt with all this in mind, Countess Spencer submitted a report in 1801, which described her recent scheme for St Albans. It had provided for support, not only in times of poor harvests and wars, but during severe winters when work was scarce. She provided very excellent salt beef and rice at very reasonable rates to poor families with the support of her subscribers. More poor families benefitted this way than would do so by direct donations. She asked subscribers for two pence to provide a pound of rice and two pence for a pound for beef. In this way she supported one large family of four, five or six children with two pounds of rice and one and a half pounds of beef each week for a contribution of only seven pence per week. The family would pay one shilling for this ration at three pence per pound for the rice and four pence per pound for the beef. There were four classes of ration determined by the size of the family. The scheme ran for three periods of six weeks at a time with a break of two weeks in between to stretch over the entire winter or until the hay harvest brought employment and vegetables would be coming in. The breaks, she felt, helped the poor to appreciate the scheme's value. The number of subscriptions obtained is not recorded, though the Countess claimed she had relieved between 800 and 900 families in the town and its environs. To cope with these numbers, the first class, or the large families, came on Mondays, the second on Tuesdays, the third on Wednesdays and the fourth on Thursdays. Some came from 5, 6 or 7 miles distant, too far to be eligible for support, but, so as not to disappoint them, those from the furthest distance still received a ticket for the one day. In the report the Countess says that she still suffered a loss herself, since she paid a woman a farthing a pound for measuring the rice and a halfpenny a pound for cutting and weighing the beef. There was also a loss on the beef bones, though they could be made into soup, which could be sold.

She had calculated that half a guinea given to a large family, or just three shillings to a poor widow, would be gone within less than one month, whereas under her scheme, the same outlay would provide support from January to June. One family, having become too low to work, told her that having good food for a while had enabled them to work again.

Her Industrial School also encouraged self-help in that the girls' sewing work was sold to pay for materials and the girls' clothes. She took this idea from her friend Mrs Sarah Trimmer, who also ran such schools, though neither was successful in making their schools self-sustaining.

Friendly Societies

Self-help was the motivation for the forming of friendly societies, at first supported by philanthropic patrons, though later mutual societies, often for specific purposes, such as funeral expenses. Most of these were male societies and also social. St Albans' Benefit and Annuity Society, founded in 1812, met annually on St Albans Day in June, at the Blue Boar Inn in Market Place, when 'an excellent dinner is provided and the invigorating glass is circulated with the most loyal sentiments and the conviviality and pleasure of the day is increased with numerous patriotic and national songs'. The monthly contributions provided sickness benefit, a sum on death and fifteen pounds per annum widows' annuity, unless they remarried.

The government encouraged such societies and passed the Friendly Societies Act of 1793[17] which suggested,

> Funds for the mutual relief and maintenance of the members in sickness, old age, and infirmity, [are] likely to be attended with very beneficial effects by promoting the happiness of individuals and at the same time diminishing the public burdens.

There were tax advantages, but each society was first to exhibit its rules in writing to the justices in Quarter Sessions, which, signed by the Clerk of the Peace, would be filed with the Session Rolls. The Liberty of St Albans records include entries for societies in almost all communities in West Hertfordshire.

The earlier, patron-led, societies included many for women, which provided education and encouraged moral behaviour. Also social, they did not attract the criticism the men's mutual societies sometimes did for their patronage of local hostelries at great cost and their members' morally dubious behaviour.

A newspaper of 1773 described the annual event of the Lichfield female society, founded three years earlier, when nearly 100 of its young women members 'neatly dressed in White, with Shepherdesses Crooks in their Hands' processed from the Guildhall to a service at the Cathedral Church. They were preceded by two of the Clergy, their Apothecary, and the Clerk of the Society, each also carrying a crook and afterwards returned to the hall where the Chief Magistrates joined them for a dinner. Dancing continued until ten o'clock.

Mrs Catherine Cappe's female society at Barwick in Elmet near Leeds had a distinctly religious flavour. Cappe was the wife of a Unitarian clergyman. From 1778, she sought to offer an alternative to the lengthy commitment of the apprenticeship system as the only way to adult employment in service for the girls, by offering training and encouragement of 'charity, good will, and piety amongst the members, that it may become an essential blessing to all, in proportion as the interests of the next world are of greater importance than the interests of this'.

Quaker philanthropist Mrs Priscilla Wakefield's society, set up in 1798, for the benefit of women and children at Tottenham High Cross, aimed to reduce resort to the services of pawnbrokers, by offering loans of between five and thirty shillings, to be repaid in small monthly payments. Loans were at the discretion of the six stewardesses, two of whom would be benefitted members. They were, however, only for purchases at wholesale prices, materials for work, articles for sale, a pig, or anything likely to produce a profit. Boys and girls could deposit small sums in a savings bank against a later apprenticeship fee, or clothing, when going in to service. Their money would be returned to the child's parents in the event of death. Members met monthly and notorious irregularity of conduct would incur expulsion.

The scheme was seen to have reciprocal advantages. The affluent would become familiar with the character, wants and resources of the indigent and thus become better qualified to afford them judicious relief and to distinguish between the deserving and the worthless. The poor, on the other hand, would be encouraged in economy and industry and the children, depositing their pittances, would be stimulated to earn and save that which would otherwise be idly spent. 'It all teaches the beneficiaries the value of character and the esteem of those, who by the dispensation of providence, are placed above them.' A report observed that more than sixty children were bringing their small treasure monthly and benefitted members were repaying their loans regularly; also that kind attention and active sympathy were being exerted by the opulent.

The St Albans Female Friendly Society

Countess Spencer founded the St Albans Female Friendly Society in 1802. Not unlike the others, it offered honorary memberships to the local wealthy at ten shillings and six pence annually, or eight guineas for life, which supported benefit members in times of sickness, lying-in and old age. Benefit members would pay three pence per week with entrance money according to their age: twelve to fifteen-year olds paid nothing, fifteen to thirty five-year olds paid from one shilling to seven shillings and six pence, whilst married women and those over thirty-five paid ten shillings and six pence.

Women of all ages could join and subscriptions rose with age. Married women paid a premium, reflecting a probable higher household income as well as a likely greater cost to the society in benefits from frequent lying-in. The Abbey parish burial register for 1804 records the passing of forty-year-old Jane Scourfield, 'the first from the Friendly Society'. She was from a family of saddlers in Holywell Ward with eight young children.

The society's honorary members were given tokens designed and produced by Matthew Boulton of Birmingham. The choice of Boulton for the purpose may reflect the connection the Gapes had with him. Elizabeth Vernon Gape, wife of Revd James Carpenter Gape, vicar of St Michael's parish and also sometime mayor of the town, was the daughter of John Fothergill, Boulton's business partner, himself a St Albans man.

John Philip was the designer and the ledger at the Soho Manufactory records the price of 200 medals as ten pounds with a further £2.12.6 for the dies. Each medal was to show the member's number and this is shown on Philip's two designs as 200, presumably notionally indicating the highest number expected.

The token held by the St Albans Museums Service shows no number, so it was perhaps a sample. The British Museum has another token and Soho House in Birmingham still has the die from which they were cast.

Solomon Shaw's *History of Verulam and St Albans*, published in 1815, describes the society's benefits, which were very similar to those at Tottenham, with the addition of assistance for lying-in women, but no children's savings bank. He regarded benefit members' contributions as paltry, less than four pence a week. At the time of his writing, the funds stood at £3,000. The society was run by a committee of ladies and if income exceeded expenditure, the overplus was to be invested responsibly.

The Countess remained patroness until her death in 1814. There was apparently no natural local successor and by 1828, the Countess's son, 2nd Earl Spencer, concerned that funds then were unlikely to cover potential claims, proposed the society be wound up. He seems not to have been a trustee, and had, by then, little interest in the town, though he may have felt obliged financially.

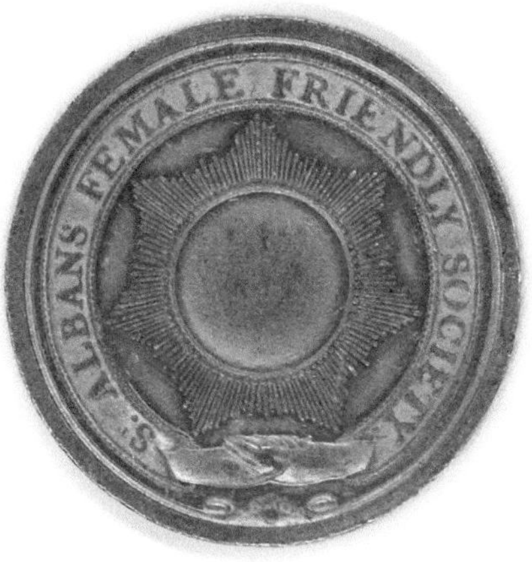

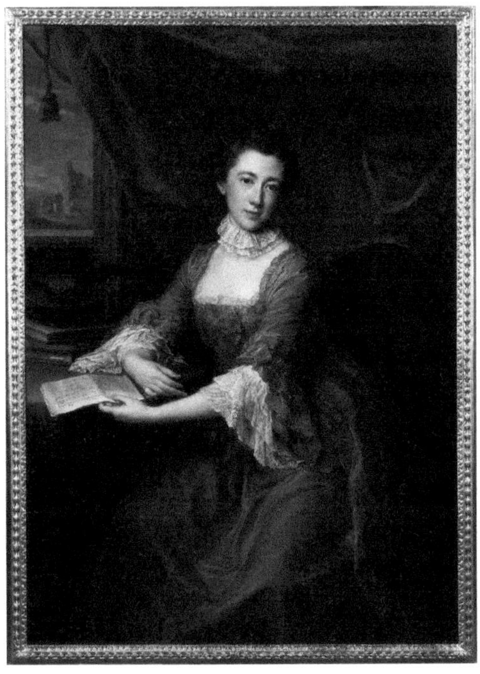

Above: St Albans Female Friendly Society token held by St Albans Museum Service. (SAMS)

Right: Georgiana Poyntz, wife of the 1st Earl Spencer, by Pompeo Batoni. (Photographic reproduction of a portrait held at Althorp.)

The loss of the Countess' personal influence may have led to a reduction in honorary membership, but from the young age of some members in 1828, it is clear there was no shortage of new benefit members. There is no list of the honorary members, although those attending a committee meeting shortly before the society's dissolution include Mrs W. Gape, Mrs Nicholson, Mrs Lipscomb, Mrs Cherry, Mrs West, Mrs Bowen and Miss Bowen, all from leading families in the town.

A special meeting of the society's committee was held on 12 June 1828 at Mrs Gape's house in St Peter's Street to discuss the Earl's proposal, and this was attended by Revd H. Small, rector of the Abbey Church, Revd Chas M. Norman, vicar of St Peter's, Revd Charles Spencer Bourchier, vicar of Sandridge, all, with the mayor of the day, trustees of the society, Treasurer Thomas Foreman Gape, and several ladies of the families mentioned above.[18]

Messrs Gape and Small put forward the proposal and the calculations of actuary Henry Smith of the Eagle Life Insurance Company, which showed a likely shortfall on the potential benefit claims of some £3,000. It was agreed a meeting of the membership should be called on 30 June at the town hall, with a view to winding up the society and distributing the present capital by way of compensation to benefit members.

The society had been constituted according to the law and its dissolution was equally formally arranged. One hundred and twenty-five copies of a notice calling the plenary meeting were printed by William Langley, stationer and bookseller on High Street at fifteen shillings and a man was paid to distribute them to the outlying villages of Sandridge, Harpenden and Redbourn.

At the meeting, the membership was in agreement with the dissolution, since their compensation would amount to a considerable sum in the hand, though one, a Mrs Sarah Palmer, held out for an annuity instead. Mrs Palmer was already a pensioner, and was persuaded subsequently that a full distribution was the way forward. It was fortuitous for her family, since the poor lady died the following year.

The Deed of Dissolution was drawn up with a final account and all benefit members signed or made their mark. This document suggested that the society was founded only in 1810, an error probably relating to the absence of any record of the rules having been exhibited in the required manner before that year, or indeed since. The Roll of the St Albans Quarter Sessions for Epiphany 1811 510 /7 records a payment of ten shillings for 'Exhibiting and recording rules, orders and regulation of a Society of Good Fellowship at the St Christopher' and 'The like for the Female Society under the patronage of the Dowager Lady Spencer ten shillings'. Whilst ten shillings was paid at intervals for exhibiting the Good Fellowship's rules at, variously, The George, the Flower de Luce, the Boar, and the Christopher, the Female Society figures in the records only that once. Perhaps the Countess regarded engagement with the inns in the town as irrelevant to her business, as she ran all her various philanthropic and community activities very personally.

The final account statement shows that there was a subcommittee which determined the benefits to be allowed and that the society's secretary had received a salary of twenty pounds per annum.

The legal fees for the dissolution of the society were twenty-three pounds seven shillings and six pence and the investigation of the affairs of the society from its inception had cost ten pounds. Three guineas were spent on presents for the clerks at Messrs Drummonds, presumably the London bankers, and at Martineau and Story, a local bank. The total sum distributed at dissolution was £4,020.18. 8 ½d. Only seventy pounds and eleven shillings had been distributed for pensions for the preceding half year, which suggests a pension of approximately nine pounds per annum. The compensation paid out to the fifteen pensioners at dissolution was £1,050.00.00, which gave an average sum of seventy pounds to each. Although at the lower end of the distribution fifteen benefit members received only ten pounds or under, the payments must have represented a considerable bonus for most members, and that several were found to marry within a year or two suggests that it offered them a substantial dowry.

The names of all the 115 Benefit members and their husbands, if married, or a parent, if under age, give a snapshot of a section of the community at that time rarely available today. In the six months prior to dissolution, eight new members had joined the society, so it clearly still attracted membership. One girl was only fourteen years old, so could have been a member for only two years at most.

The society had clearly flourished, though the town's population of a little more than 3,000, did not support it as Lichfield, a town of only 2,500, had done with, in 1801, two such societies with a combined membership of 240 young women.

From the names of the St Albans members, the few parents and the sixty-one men named, it has been possible to reconstruct the families and establish the class of society of the membership.

Eighty of the women and their men have been traced with some degree of certainty. Of the remainder, there is no apparent record, other than their membership of the society. This reflects the unreliability of both registration and census records, as much as the mobility or longevity of the women. The pensioners were, with one exception, all still in their sixties, and strangely, nearly all died in the following decade. The largest number of members (twenty-five) came from the town itself but five came from Sandridge, seven from Redbourn and the remainder from Tittenhanger, Sleapshyde, Bricket Wood, Harpenden and other outlying areas. Three lived in almshouses, two in Marlborough Buildings and one at Raynshaws in Spicer Street. The occupations of sixteen of the menfolk mentioned or otherwise traced were found to be agricultural labourers, two were gardeners, one was the sexton at St Peter's and two were, later in life, farm bailiffs. Successive census records provide a view of both upwards and downwards social mobility of those recorded as either labourers or agricultural labourers in youth. Few women's occupations were given, though several have been found from other records to have been straw plaiters. One was a laundress and one, later, in widowhood, became a schoolmistress. Seventy of the women or their male representative could not sign their name, making only a mark on the final accounts.

The Countess also ran a small loan scheme for women, which may not have been part of the Friendly Society arrangements. Entries in the small indexed notebook she used to record loans begin in 1802, close to the date the society was established, although there is no reference to the society in the book.[19] Some loans in 1802 were to women who appeared on the society's dissolution document of 1828,[20] twenty-six years later, so the two schemes did benefit the same section of the community. Loans were also recorded to her chaplain,

Revd James Preedy, and her daughter, Georgiana Duchess of Devonshire, and there was one to [William] Wells, a local carpenter.

Friendly Societies thrived and expanded throughout the nineteenth century, acknowledged as the usual form of insurance against all eventualities. From the formation of societies designed to buy and then redistribute small parcels of building land with a view to increasing the franchise, which was mostly dependent on property ownership, the movement grew to include Building Societies. Savings banks, designed to encourage prudence on the part of the less well off, were introduced, one with branches across Hertfordshire, and these replaced the small loan schemes some Friendly Societies offered, a service now more commonly offered by Credit Unions. The education the Female Societies promoted was overtaken by more direct provision of schools for all. There seems to have been no successor in St Albans to Countess Spencer's society, though many other communities in the county did later form Female Friendly Societies, perhaps on the more mutual basis that the men's societies favoured.

8. Local Occupations and Activities

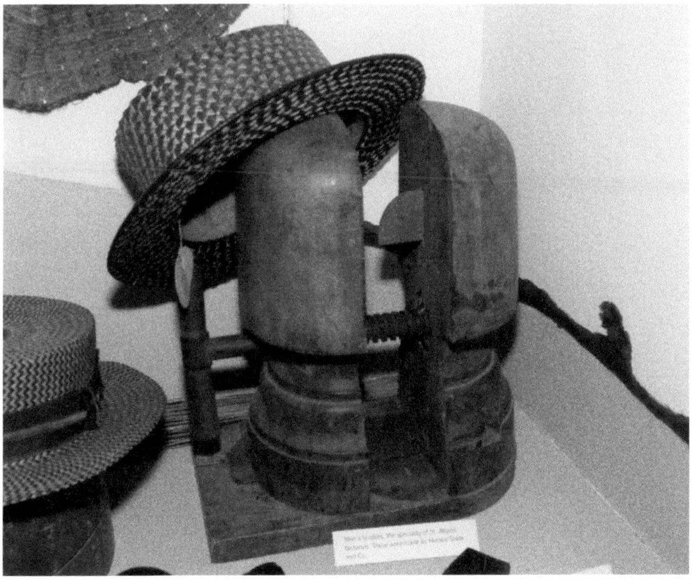

Women and children plaited the straw for the many hat factories in the town. (SAMS)

St Albans has always been a commuter town, which suggests that the economic activity of its residents has been elsewhere. True enough, with London on its doorstep, but St Albans has also always had a degree of self-sufficiency.

An interesting variety of industries have been based in the town and domestic service and the hospitality trade, the straw plait and hat trades and agriculture, have offered a range of possibilities for women.

The river provided power for mills which produced silk, cotton and paper as well as grinding corn. Its water also supported the leather trades, diamond polishing and the watercress industry and springs have been used to bottle drinking water.

Diamonds – Not Always for Ever!

Diamond polishing is perhaps the most surprising of these industries. The waterworks at Sopwell, described elsewhere, having failed, its site was, at least from 1765, used by London diamond polisher Henry Potter. His work and financial support came from the agent Moses Machorro of Leadenhall Street, who traded the diamonds sent back by successful merchants and administrators of the East India Company, including Robert Clive, famed for his victory at the Battle of Plassey and thus taking control for Britain of most of India. Sometime after Potter's death in January 1779, the site was taken up

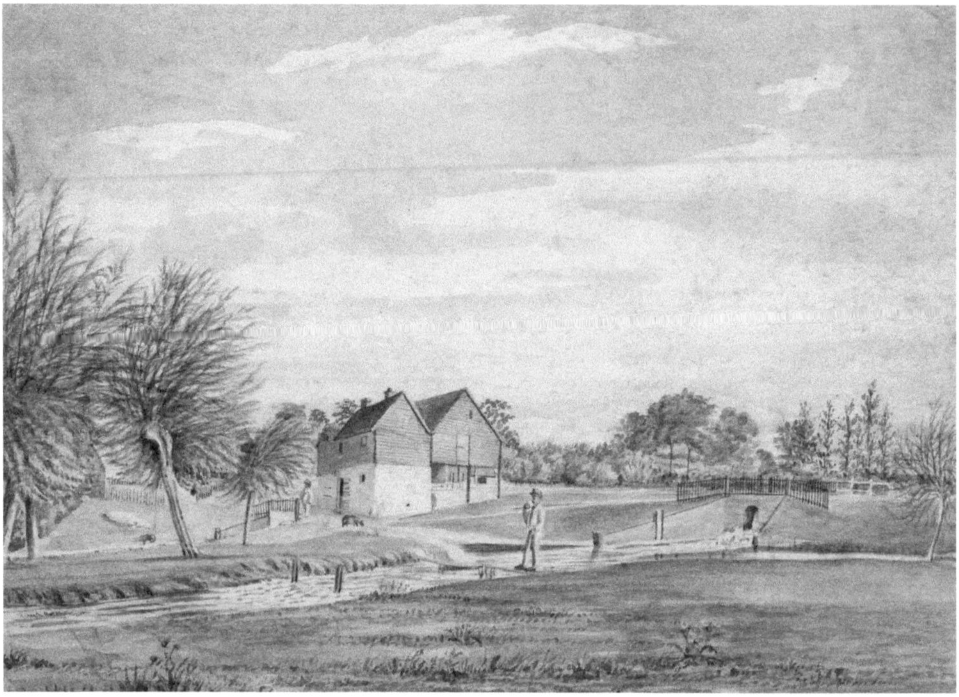

The Cotton Mill by J. H. Buckingham. (SAMS)

by cotton merchants Maxey and Gill, who built a new mill for the production of cotton candlewick. This was a big operation for which they brought parish apprentices to the town from London.

Bottled Water

The purity of the town's spring water was exploited by pharmaceutical chemist Henry Gilham Martin. His shop was in the Market Place, but in 1853 he opened a manufactory to produce bottled water in White Hart Yard on Holywell Hill. Trading as Holywell Mineral Waters he offered aerated waters and other flavoured beverages. His company was followed by Francis Dunham's City Steam and Mineral Water Company almost next door at No. 51 Holywell Hill, which competition he resented. His advertisements highlighted the distinction between the two companies. Martin's factory was sold off on his death in 1886.

Political Interests

Of even more importance in the town were the political interests of the leading families in respect of the borough's right to return two representatives to parliament. Election time brought both income and excitement to the town. The Whig Spencer and Tory Grimston families vied over the two seats, though sometimes colluded. This continued until the aftermath of the election of 1807, when, having failed to secure his nominee's seat in parliament, the 2nd Earl Spencer threw in the towel and withdrew to his principal estate at Althorp and his beloved book collecting.

St Albans was privileged to have a larger than usual franchise. In addition to freemen of the borough and the owners of property, the town's ratepayers also had the vote until this was withdrawn by the Reform Act. The ratepayers expected payment for their services at election time – usually five pounds per vote.

Freemen either served apprenticeships, were the sons of freemen, or paid for their freedom, a method known as 'redemption'. However, it was also in the gift of the mayor and Corporation to grant freedoms gratis. At election time, many were granted, regardless of eligibility, as long as support was for the favoured party. In 1743 the death of the sitting MP caused a by-election. Despite an entertainment staged on the eve of the election at Gorhambury of 'near 900 persons of that Corporation',[21] it was the Duchess of Marlborough's candidate, Hans Stanley, an Opposition Whig, who triumphed, albeit with wholesale bribery and the votes of thirty-one new freemen.

However, those were troubling times and the future uncertain. The king was abroad fighting the War of Austrian Succession. The ageing Robert Walpole had been defeated as prime minister and the Jacobites were threatening. Perhaps to ensure a different outcome at the earliest opportunity, in the following months a further 300 outsiders were granted freedoms. Mayor, surgeon Joseph Handley, agent for James West, the Grimston representative, was taking no chances.

Canvassing during elections was a very public affair and a great entertainment in the town. For musicians it meant work, playing all over the town for the candidates, and then for the winner of the election. For the inns providing headquarters for rival parties, there was much business and money flowed.

The mayor was the returning officer for elections. Hustings were set up in front of the Clock Tower, and after nominations and speeches, a show of hands could determine the outcome. If this was disputed, then a poll took place, which took several days. The votes were recorded by the town clerk and later published in a bound book. Secret ballot was introduced only in 1872.

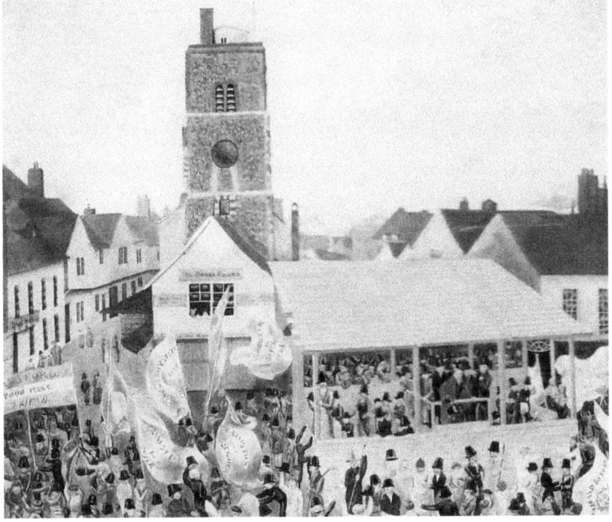

The hustings for the General Election of January 1835 painted by Emma, the young daughter of the then mayor and returning officer, lawyer and banker Richard William Brabant. (SAMS)

DID YOU KNOW?

The family of Diana, Princess of Wales, had a controlling interest in St Albans throughout the eighteenth century. The generosity of the 1st Earl Spencer, and later his widow, ensured the loyalty of the townspeople to the family at election time. The 2nd Earl was mayor of St Albans in 1790 and High Steward from 1783 to 1807.

Passing Visitors

As well as travellers passing through the town, many came for the Court Sessions for both the Borough and the Liberty of St Albans, and yet more for the three annual fairs. The latter took place at Lady Day, Michaelmas and the middle of June. There were more stalls than on regular market days, and the Michaelmas Fair, known as the Statty or Statute Fair, was where young agricultural and other servants fixed new contracts of employment. Since the balance of their wages was paid at the end of a previous contract, money flowed on drink and entertainment at the fair. The fair in June was for horses and other animals.

The popularity of the eighteenth-century Grand Tour brought both a taste for the classical styles and interest in antiquity. On his visit to the town in 1721, Revd William Stukeley mapped what he found of both Roman Verulamium and the medieval monastery, and this stimulated interest in the town.

In 1729 a newspaper noted that 'three figures in basso-relievo representing the martyrdom of Amphibalus, who converted Alban to Christianity, were discovered in a subterranean room excavated in the Abbey Orchard'.

With lively hostelries, thriving shops, and the various churches, the town had much to offer both those passing through as well as visitors in the town for business or pleasure.

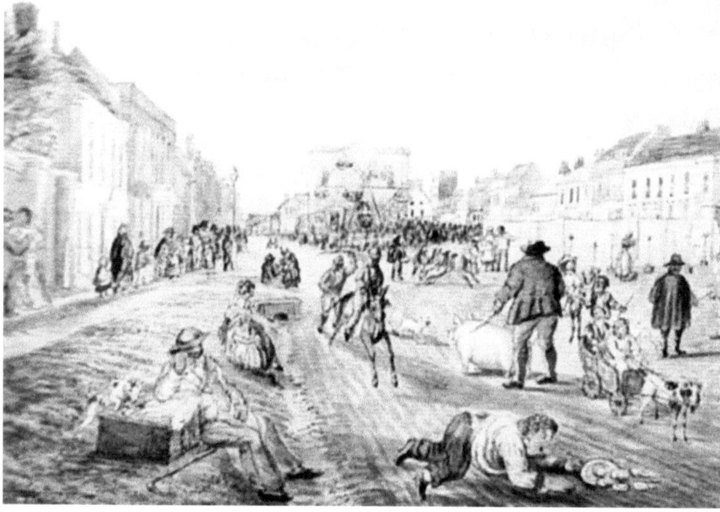

Michaelmas Fair 1852, with fairground entertainments in front of the town hall by J. H. Buckingham. (SAMS)

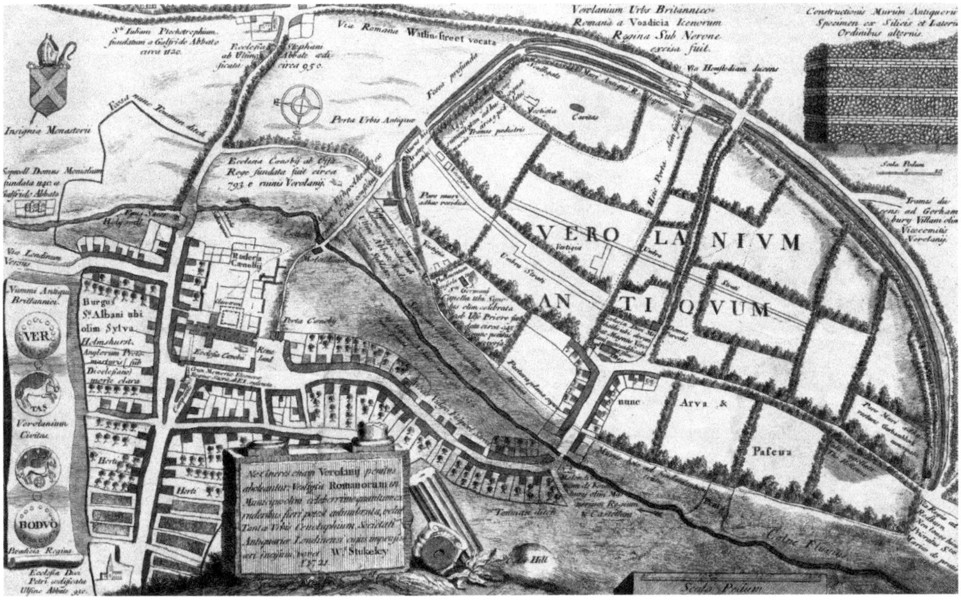

Plan of St Albans and Verulamium drawn up by Revd Dr William Stukeley in 1721. (SAMS)

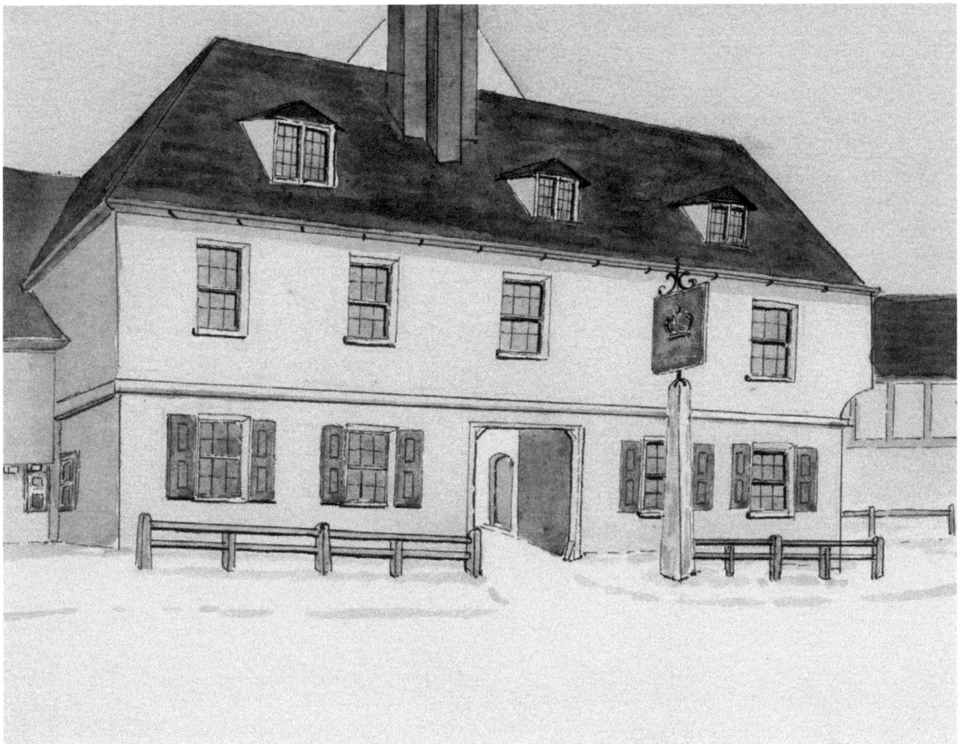

Watercolour copy by H. R. Wilton Hall of an original sketch by Pridmore *c.* 1800 of the Crown Inn on Holywell Hill. (SAMS)

Hugh Bolton took over the Crown Inn on the north corner of Sopwell Lane into Holywell Hill in 1737 and boasted that 'all Travellers, as well as the accustomed Guests, may be sure to have good Entertainment and civil Usage'. He had on display 'for the Entertainment of the Curious ... several Pieces of Antiquity, which were Dug out of the Ruins of the Ancient City of Verulam, and the Monastery of St Albans'.

In 1782, naturalist and antiquarian Thomas Pennant, in his *Journey from Chester to London*, recalls calling in at Lord Grimston's newly built Palladian mansion at Gorhambury. A stately home was often, then as now, opened to the public, especially when the family were absent for the Season. The servants remaining would be happy to show visitors round for a small fee. Pennant comments on the fine collection of portraits there, which had been transferred from Nicholas Bacon's Tudor mansion nearby.

The vast Abbey Church itself was a considerable attraction. The excavation for a vault for the Gape family, on the death of eighty-nine-year-old John, a former MP for the town, in 1703, had led to the rediscovery of the tomb of the Royal Duke Humphrey of Gloucester, who died in 1447. When the duke's lead coffin was opened, it was found to contain his corpse, embalmed in a brown liquor. This became the subject of much fascination for visitors and was soon presumed to have special anti-ageing properties. Actor David Garrick, a regular visitor to the town, deplored what he regarded as a waste of good liquor on a corpse, and, staying, in 1765, at the Christopher Inn with colleague James Quin, penned a soliloquy on the topic.

The tomb was cared for from 1746 until his death in 1798 by the redoubtable parish clerk, plumber and glazier John Kent. No doubt topping up the embalming liquor from

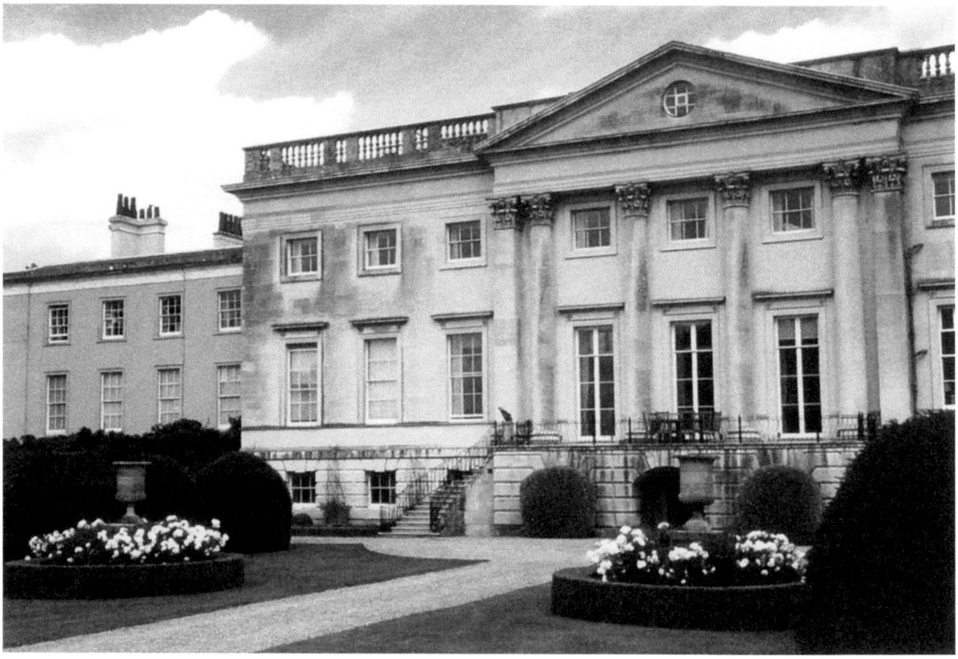

Gorhambury House. (Darnell Collection © SAHAAS)

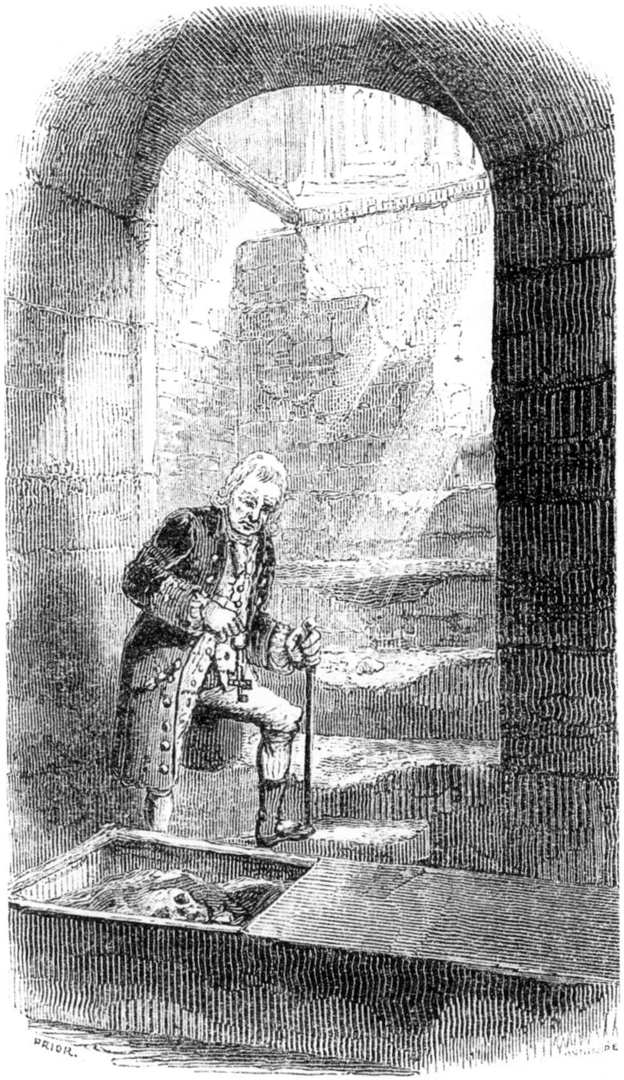

The parish clerk opens the Royal Duke Humphrey's tomb to reveal his embalmed corpse. (Courtesy of the archives at the Cathedral and Abbey Church of St Alban)

time to time with suitable spirits, he took his duties seriously and was well informed about the antiquarian past of the building and its surroundings. With the restoration work of the 1870s, the tomb was closed and only in 1999 did it become visible once more, complete with much eighteenth-century graffiti, thanks to the millennium project of the Hertfordshire Freemasons.

The Abbey Church has always been a popular wedding venue, and many from afar celebrated or affirmed their marriages there. With soldiers in their gay uniforms encamped or billeted in the town, there were also many snap weddings of local girls hoping to follow their beaux on their manoeuvres, but the girls were often disappointed, since this was not allowed. There were many baptisms and also burials of infants attributed to often anonymous soldiers.

9. Sport and Leisure

DID YOU KNOW?

Archery was popular in the nineteenth-century high society, especially among the ladies. The Hertfordshire Toxophilite Society, formed principally by Lady Verulam, met from 1827 to 1831 at the cricket ground on the north side of the town to pursue the sport and then dance the quadrille and the waltz through the evening to the music of Mr Weippert's band.

For the gentry, fox-hunting was a popular sport and provided exercise; perhaps less commonly, but spectacularly, stag chasing, the favoured sport of the German kings, was also pursued. Released from a cart at the meet, the stag would be chased until caught, then, if still in reasonable condition, taken back to its paddock to await another sporting day.

In 1788, a stag released on Farnham Common in Buckinghamshire ran round that county, passed through Watford, Hemel Hempstead and St Albans until caught at Hatfield after four and a half hours. Six horses died in that chase, though the report makes no mention of the stag. Fifty years later, a stag released on No Man's Land in 1840 ran through Harpenden, across to Childwickbury, up Verulam Road and up and down St Peter's Street before being cornered in the Peahen yard.

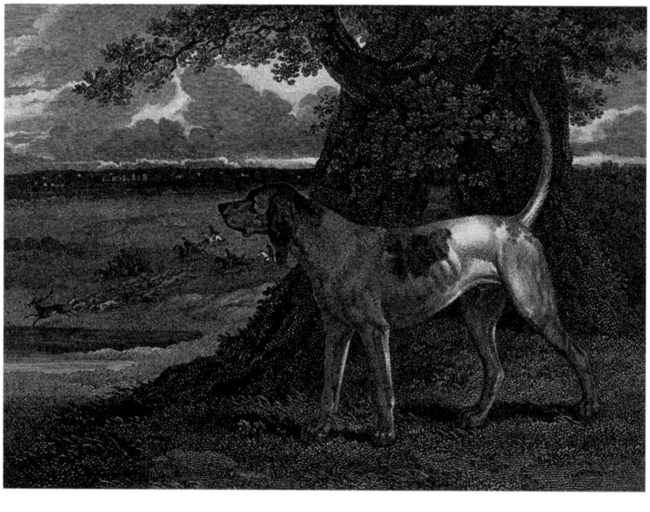

A staghound looks down on a stag chase in the valley below. Etching by J. Scott after Philip Reinagle, 1820. (Wellcome Collection)

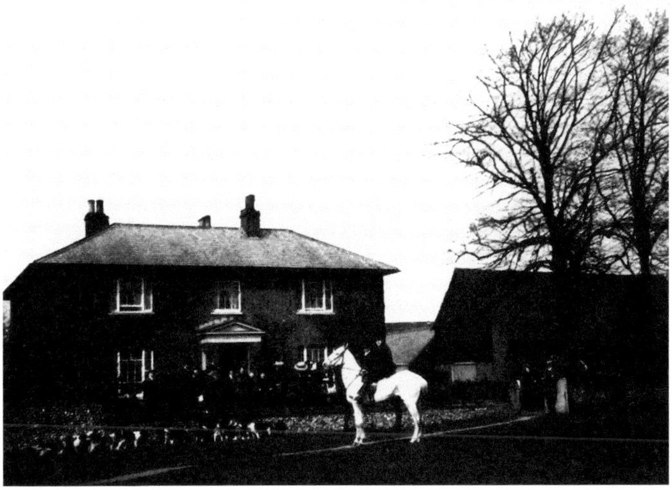

Aldenham Harriers met at Heath Farm until well into the twentieth century. (Courtesy of Chris Reynolds)

Cockfighting

Hunting, however inhumane, has always had its justification, but cockfighting was a sport purely for the excitement and the money to be made. This popular rural pastime was only outlawed in England and Wales under the Cruelty to Animals Act of 1835. A further Act of 1849 also brought to an end such cruel activities as bear-baiting, bull-running and dog-fighting. Most cockfights took place in inn yards and in 1773 a two-day main, or series of battles, of thirty-one cocks was held between the gentlemen of Buckinghamshire and Hertfordshire at the Crown Inn in St Albans. The Fighting Cocks pub on Abbey Mill Lane was first mentioned by that name in 1779, so also a likely venue for that sport.

In the early nineteenth century Tommy Coleman of the Turf Hotel in Chequer Street brought steeplechasing to the town. He arranged meets and determined the ground over

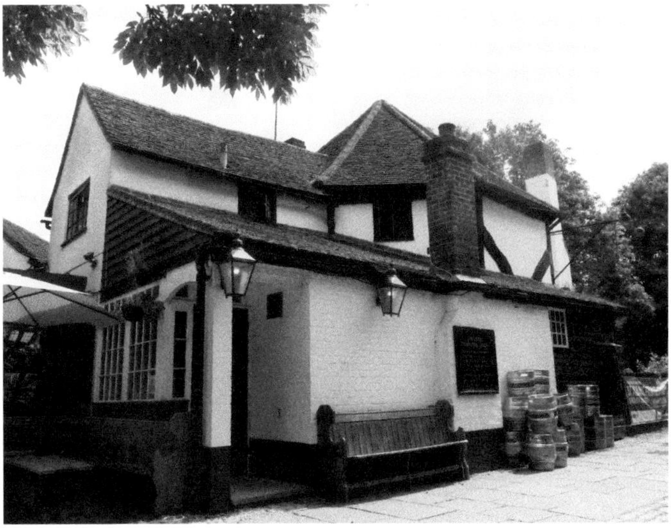

The Fighting Cocks public house. (Kari Lundgaard)

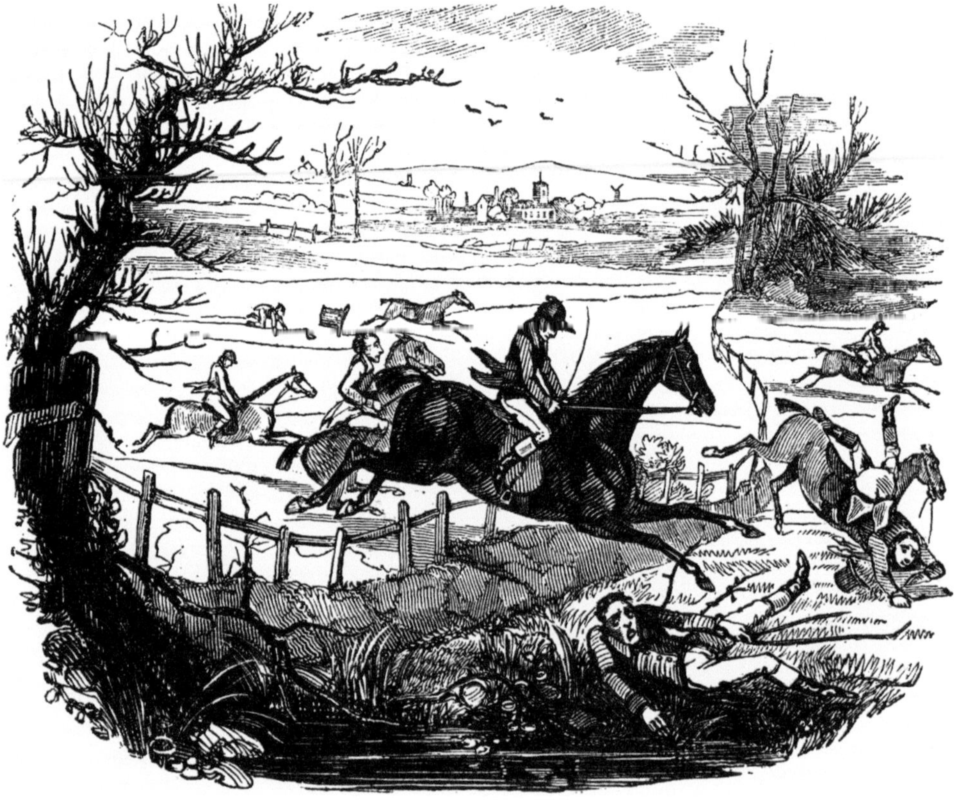

Brilliant steeplechase at St Albans in 1832 from the cover of Pierce Egan's *Book of Sports XI.* (SAMS)

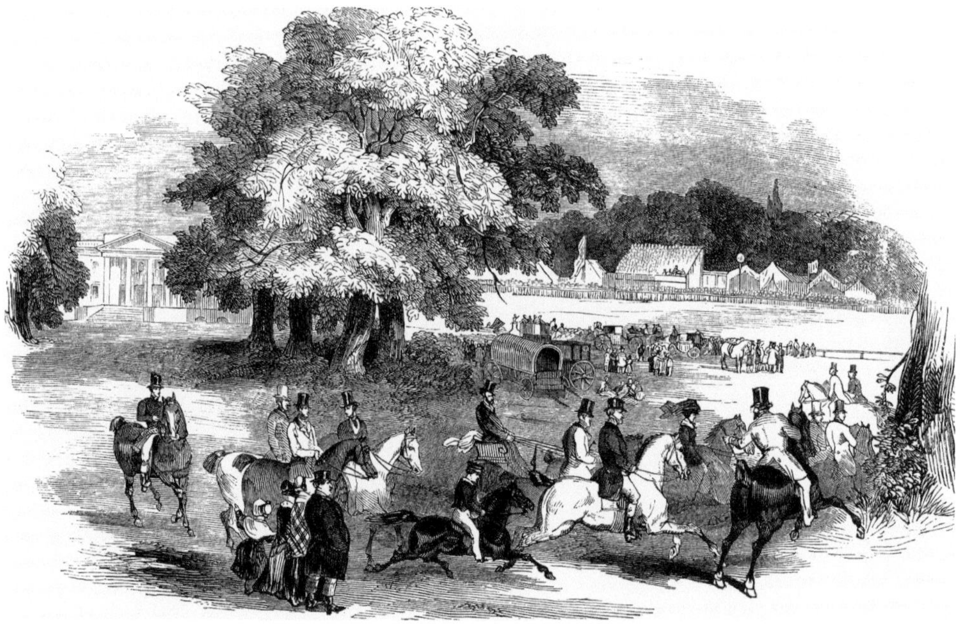

Gorhambury races, 1844. (SAMS)

which the race would run. Steeplechasing was not popular with farmers, whose land was trampled by the riders, nor the fox-hunting community, who saw their sport as both healthier and more useful. After some ten years, steeplechasing ceased in St Albans, as Liverpool's new Aintree course was developed, though flat racing continued here.

Coleman also organised boxing matches. In May 1833, the Irish champion pugilist Simon Byrne was challenged by James (Deaf) Burke to a fight for two hundred pounds, under the Broughton rules, to be held somewhere within 40 miles of London. Coleman offered to stage it at No Man's Land, conveniently out of immediate sight of the borough magistrates. The ring was fenced and all set up. The fight began, with both men in good spirits, first one on top and then the other. Bets were on the first to be downed and the first to draw blood. Journalist Solomon Shaw reported that some men broke through the fencing and stormed the ring, obstructing the work of the seconds. Pickpockets were also about and Shaw admitted being thieved himself. Any magistrate present should have stopped the event under the Riot Act, but the fight continued for three hours and six minutes and no fewer than ninety-nine rounds. Both men were by then almost completely incapable; Byrne had to be carried off, whilst Burke, who was declared the winner, could only walk with assistance.

Burke returned to the Turf Hotel, and a hot bath of which Coleman boasted there, and Byrne to the Woolpack next door to the Peahen on Holywell Hill. Surgeon Francis Kingston was called to Byrne and found him unconscious, apparently suffering from blows to his head. Rather better the next day, he told Kingston the greatest pain was to his side, but attributed his debility to having drunk too much, eaten too little and walked to the point of perspiration before the match. He had been keen to reduce his weight, which was down to 13 stone 4 pounds before the fight. His greatest concern was the ignominy of having lost to Burke. The noted surgeon Sir Astley Cooper, from Gadebridge, also attended him, but the next day, Sunday, Byrne died. The inquest, held at the inn, called for a post-mortem, which was conducted by Kingston together with colleague surgeons Lipscombe, Rogers and Webster. At the town hall, coroner Thomas Ward Blagg pronounced the jury verdict of manslaughter of Byrne by Burke with the seconds and other participants also implicated. They were all immediately arrested and trial set at Hertford. However, the verdict there was that death was not due to the blows to Byrne's head, but to other factors, and the men were all acquitted. Byrne's body, held until announcement of the verdict, was buried at the Abbey Church immediately after, it being gruesomely reported that the summer weather was already leading to decomposition. Two hundred sympathetic supporters attended the funeral, though not his destitute widow and four children, who were unable to travel from Dublin.

Burke's pugilistic career suffered considerably and, finding no other opponents, he emigrated to America to find a living there.

Archery was a sport of the rich which the ladies could join in. Favoured by the Prince of Wales as a young man, it became a social sport in the 1820s. James Grimston, now raised to the rank of Earl by his brother-in-law, Prime Minister Lord Liverpool, welcomed high society to the mansion at Gorhambury. In the summer of 1828, he held the first of several annual 'fêtes champêtres' for 200 guests. There were targets on the lawns and prizes offered for the two most successful toxophilists. Winners were the Marquis of Abercorn,

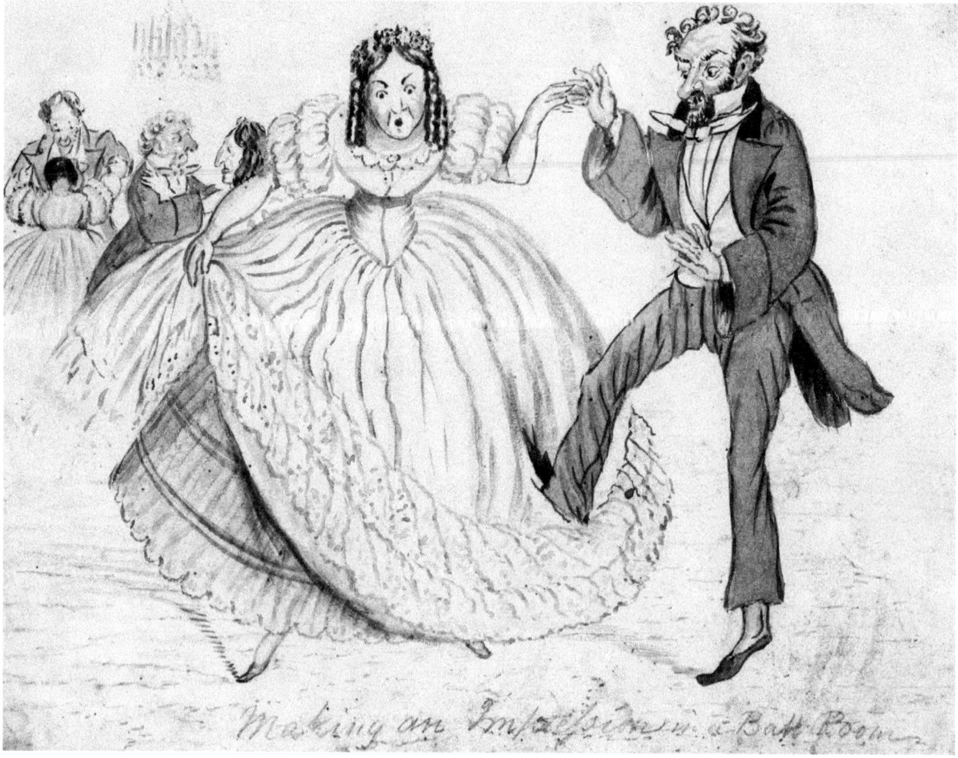

Making an Impression in the Ball Room by J. H. Buckingham. (SAMS)

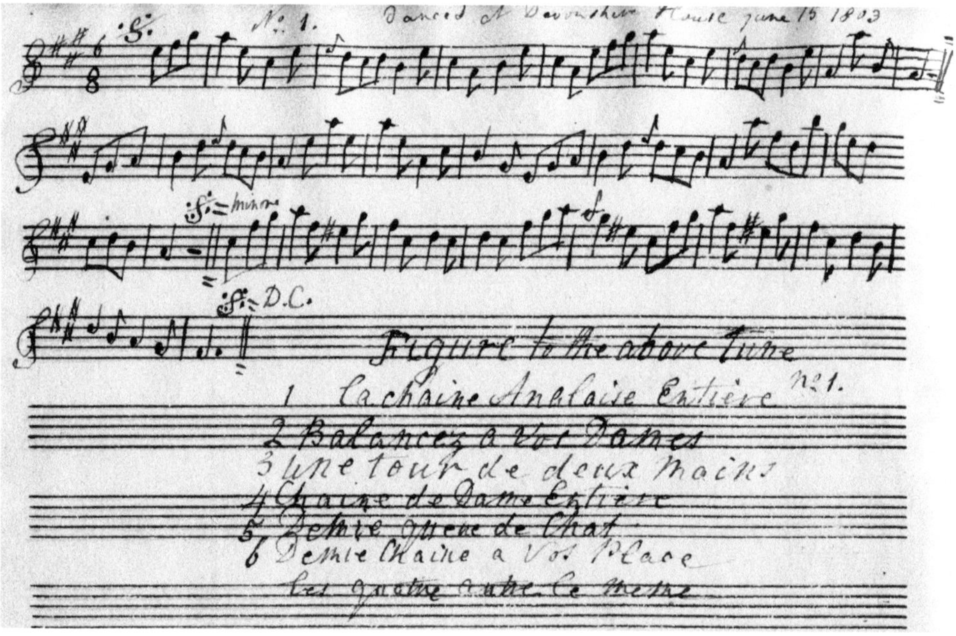

Manuscript dance music from the collection of Marianne Lawes, née Sherman, of Rothamsted. (Harpenden LHS)

and Lady Emily Grimston, daughter of the host. Afterwards a splendid repast was enjoyed in the two salons to the music of the Marquis of Salisbury's Military Band, followed by dancing in the ballroom to Mr Weippert's band. Weippert was famous for his quadrilles. This dance became popular in England and the houses of Hertfordshire after Napoleon's defeat in 1815, though was probably introduced by the Devonshire set, following the visit of Lady Elizabeth Foster, later the Duke's second wife, to Paris during the brief Peace of Amiens in 1802. Some manuscript dance music from that era survives in the hand of Merry Johnstone, the wife of John Christopher Sherman junior and mother of Marianne Lawes of Rothamsted. A note suggests dancing to that music took place at Devonshire House in June 1803.

The 'Cricketers' at the top end of St Peter's Street celebrates the fact that the Heath behind it was an early venue for cricket. The sport was taken seriously, especially by local gentlemen, such as Lord Frederick Beauclerk, vicar of St Michael's from 1827 to 1850. The local club had a fine reputation in the county, and teams from the Grammar School and elsewhere played on their ground. In 1844 a friendly match played between the senior and junior members of the club was followed by an 'evening spent convivially at the club house, the King's Head Inn'. J. H. Buckingham's drawing of a one-legged cricket match on the field below the newly built Christ Church on Verulam Road and the captions he wrote reflect such charitable matches often held in aid of army and navy veterans, typically Greenwich pensioners.

More popular amongst the ordinary people, or at least the young men, was swimming in the Ver. The deep pool at Sopwell, where the waterworks and then the cotton mill had been, became the focus of this activity. Thomas Deacon bathed in the river,

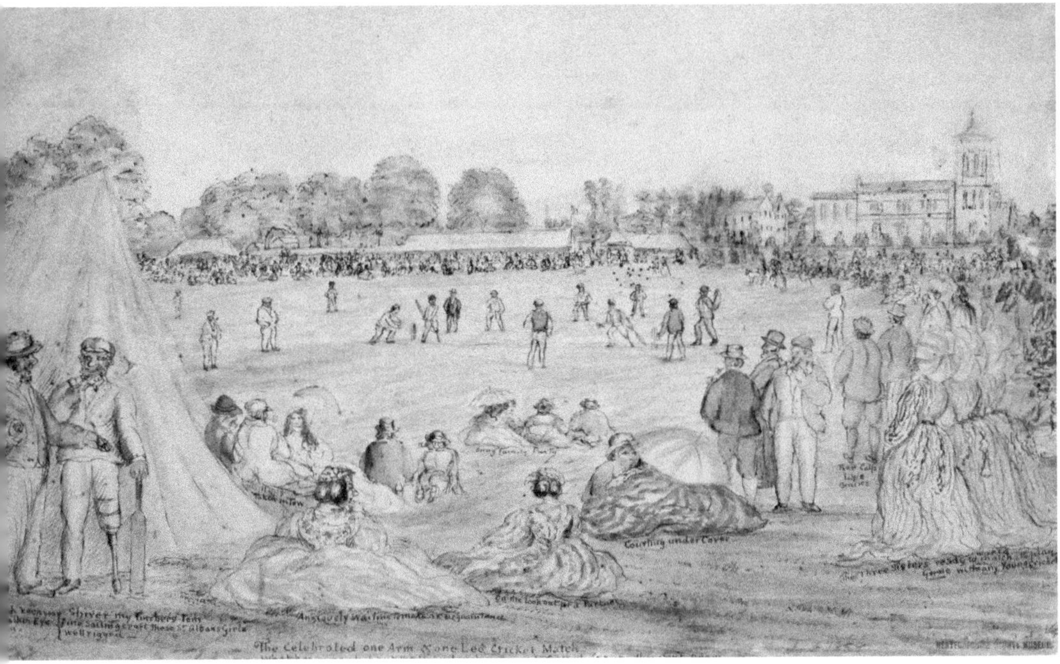

One-legged cricket match on what is now the Victoria Playing Field, by J. H. Buckingham. (SAMS)

and, in 1835, left his clothes on the bank with his watch in his hat. James Hazell, another bather, was later sentenced to three months' imprisonment, Deacon's watch having been found on his person. By 1851 it was a commercial enterprise. Wooden boards provided an edge and an attendant kept the mud on the bottom dredged, charging bathers a penny a swim and offering prizes at swimming competitions. It was claimed that 6,000 persons used the pool over a ten-week season. Not everyone however restricted themselves to the official venue for swimming. In 1871 a group of boys was brought before the bench for indecent exposure whilst bathing in the river close to a public footpath. More sober inhabitants called for a better venue in the town, describing the river as that 'dirty, weedy, shallow, polluted and narrow stream known ... as the Ver'. Long debated, the river baths were finally, in 1890, taken over by the Corporation and, later, replaced with a properly built swimming pool.

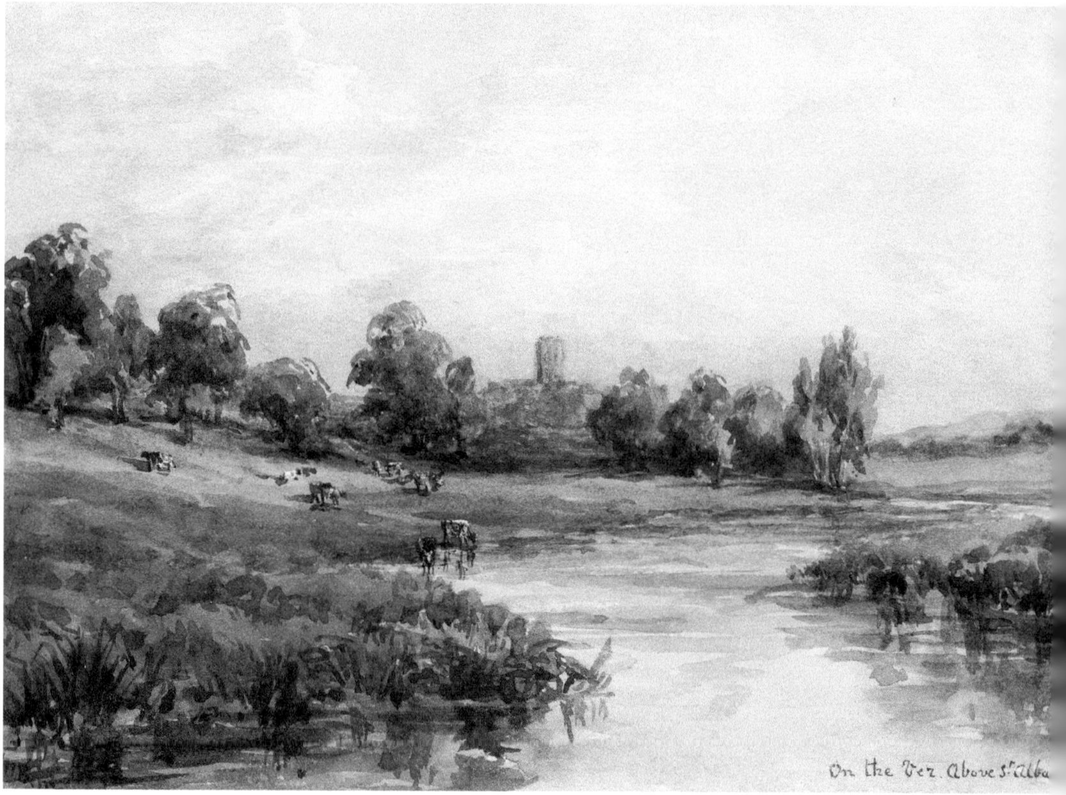

Painting of the River Ver between Redbourn and St Albans. (SAMS)

10. Entertainment

The gentry houses around the town were grand enough for entertaining both family and visitors. Reports of the family life enjoyed by the Marlboroughs at Holywell House in the early eighteenth century and the Dowager Countess Spencer there four generations later, reveal that their private chaplains and domestic companions would read to them, that they 'played much at chess, whist, piquet, and ombre ... and took great delight in the performance of private theatricals'. Some houses were specifically designed with entertainment in mind.[22] Inns sometimes became residential. Alderman, and by then Dr, Joseph Handley took on the former Red Lion Inn. This was nearer to the then very narrow entrance from the Market Place to George Street than the later built Great Red Lion, now occupied by the Zizzi restaurant. In 1762, the Turnpike Trustees authorised a lamp to be placed on this dangerous corner to reduce the many accidents which occurred there. Handley marked the occasion of George III's accession to the throne in 1761 by treating the 'numerous members of the gentry who favoured him with a visit to his house'

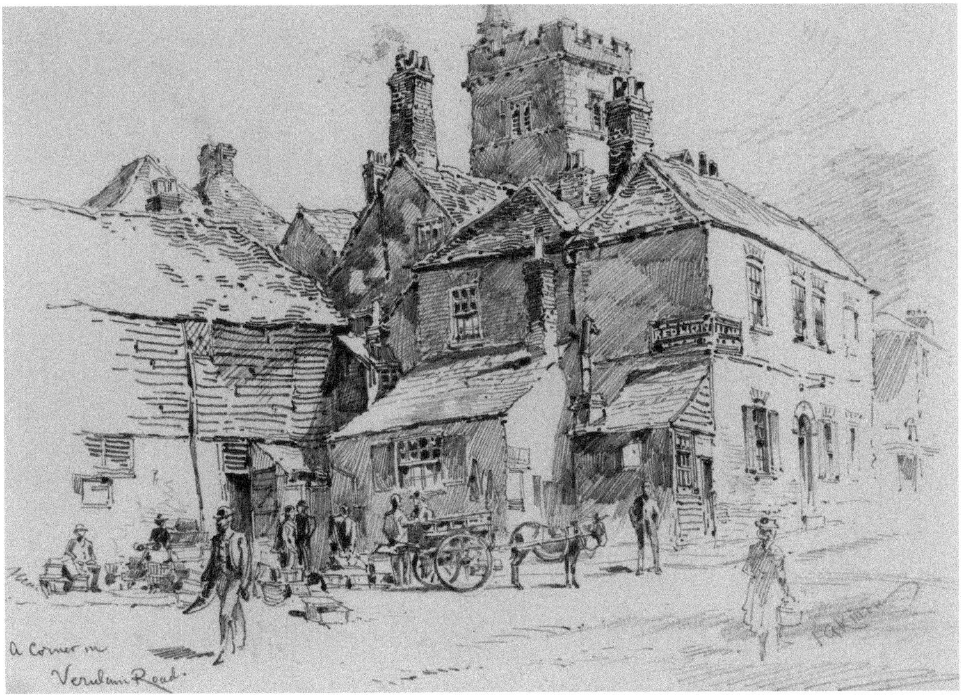

Drawing by F. G. Kitton of the old Red Lion Inn, as rebuilt in 1799. The site is the Zizzi restaurant today. (SAMS)

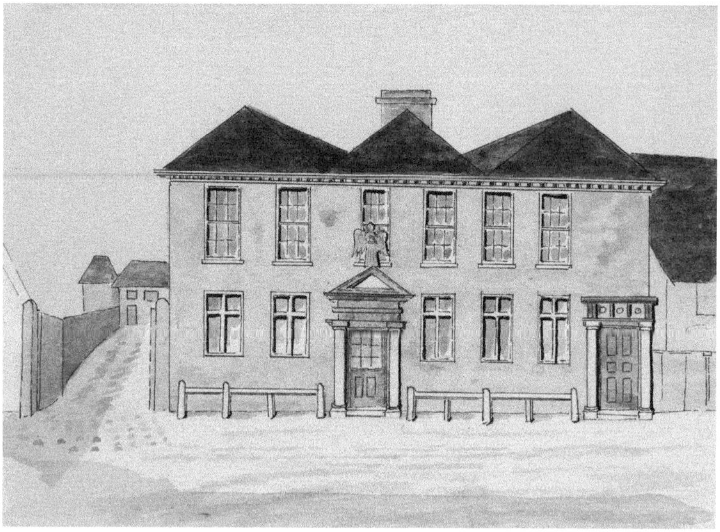

The Angel Inn, Fishpool Street, St Albans. Watercolour copied in 1907 by H. R. Wilton Hall from an original sketch by Pridmore *c.* 1800. (SAMS)

with wine, punch, good beer and English roast beef, as well as providing strong beer for the populace. Then he entertained the whole town with 'the finest set of fireworks ever exhibited in this place', all at his own expense. This was certainly lavish even in those highly politically charged times.

Inns were venues for meetings and feasts, but only in 1747 was there also an assembly room in the town, when Joseph Jackson opened his Angel Inn on Fishpool Street. He catered for coaches passing through as well as the needs of locals, but more importantly could provide for public breakfasting and dancing. There could now be a Season in St Albans.

In 1773, in a letter to his absent wife, Lord Grimston wrote of an event which could well have taken place at the Angel:

> I am going this evening to the much-celebrated St Albans Ball where I suppose I shall exhibit as Master of Ceremonies, and probably sport a minuet for the benefit of Mr Sherman [a local musician] and some despairing miss who dies to make a figure'[23]

Georgiana, Duchess of Devonshire and her sister, Harriet, Countess Bessborough, visited the Angel during the election campaign of 1784. Seeking votes for the candidate of their brother, the 2nd Earl Spencer, amongst the farmers and traders there, according to letters to the family, they found the local gentry less than inspiring company!

Fishpool Street was bypassed by the new Verulam Road in 1823, which brought the demise of The Angel, but soon after, the construction of the Regency building now our museum and gallery provided a replacement. This was primarily a courthouse, but included space for town hall activities and an assembly room. An expensive building, it was intended to establish St Albans as the county town at a time when reform was in the air and the various county authorities likely to merge. Local resident James Brown, a correspondent for the *Gentleman's Magazine*, observed:

> Our Magistrates have built us a new court House, well executed – acknowledged – but supposed to have cost the Liberty of St Albans, about £14,000 – and confessed near half as big again as there was any occasion for; the true object of which seems to have been, to out-vie Hertford, & to provide a Ball Room for the Ladies, 60 feet long.[24]

The new assembly room was, however, well used for musical events and also lectures and other social events. Lecturers there included, in 1836, James Quilter Rumball FRCS, who maintained an asylum at Oster House, on phrenology – that 'beautiful, interesting but abstruse science'. Rumball lectured to more than seventy of the most respectable ladies and gentlemen of the town. Still popular in 1849, 'Mr Matthews' came to deliver more on that subject.

Such lectures provided a new opportunity for an outing for society women, and a reporter observed on Rumball's lecture how pleasing it was to witness such a display of

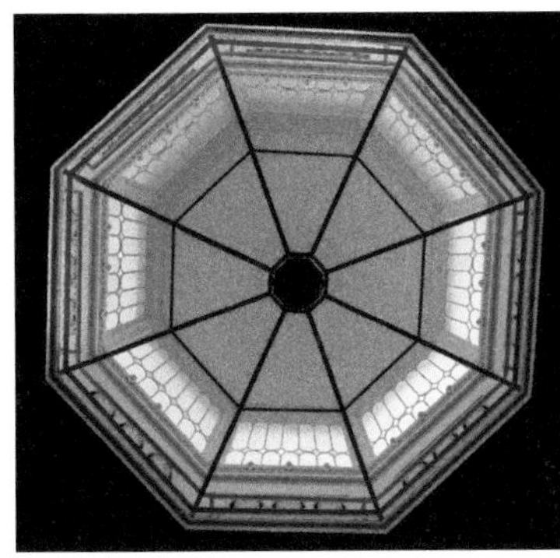

Right: Atrium of the courtroom built in 1831. (Kari Lundgaard)

Below: St Albans town hall in 2009, before its opening as the town's museum and gallery. (Darnell Collection © SAHAAS)

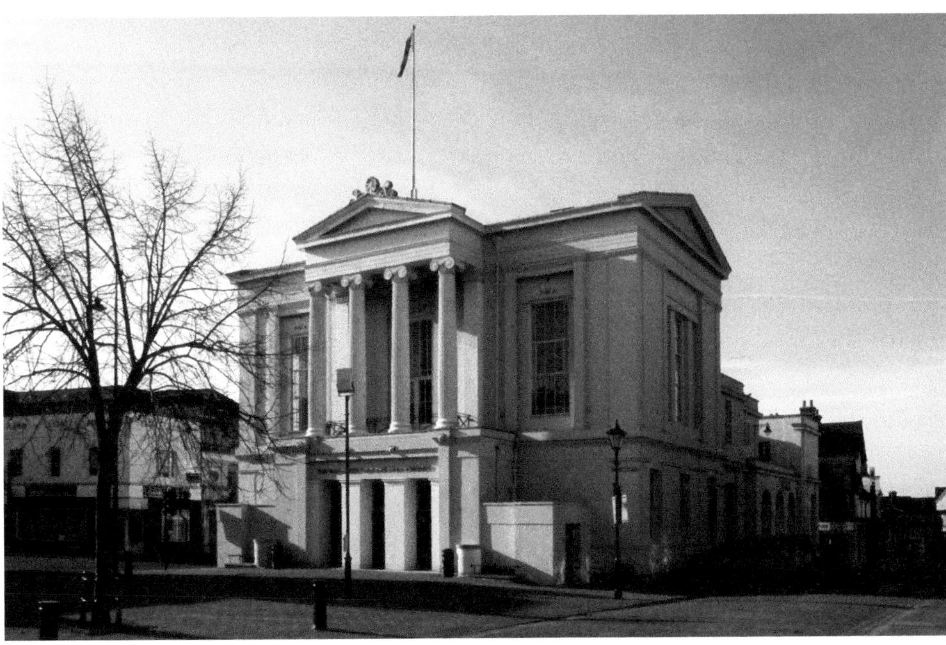

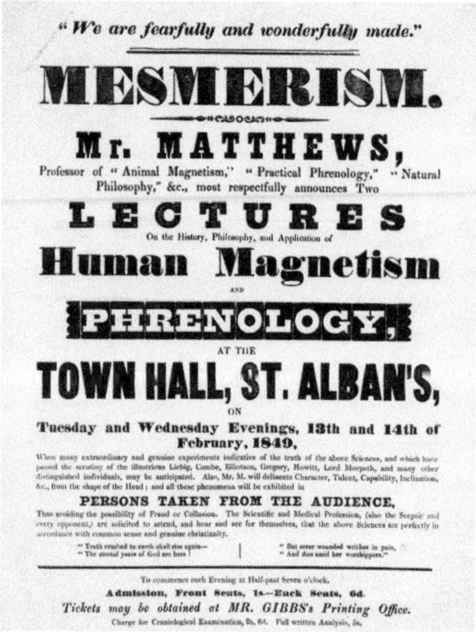

"We are fearfully and wonderfully made."

MESMERISM.

Mr. MATTHEWS,

Professor of "Animal Magnetism," "Practical Phrenology," "Natural Philosophy," &c., most respectfully announces Two

LECTURES

On the History, Philosophy, and Application of

Human Magnetism

AND

PHRENOLOGY,

AT THE

TOWN HALL, ST. ALBAN'S,

ON

Tuesday and Wednesday Evenings, 13th and 14th of February, 1849,

When many extraordinary and genuine experiments indicative of the truth of the above Sciences, and which have passed the scrutiny of the illustrious Liebig, Combe, Elliotson, Gregory, Howitt, Lord Morpeth, and many other distinguished individuals, may be anticipated. Also, Mr. M. will delineate Character, Talent, Capability, Inclination, &c., from the shape of the Head; and all these phenomena will be exhibited in

PERSONS TAKEN FROM THE AUDIENCE,

Thus avoiding the possibility of Fraud or Collusion. The Scientific and Medical Profession, (also the Sceptic and every opponent,) are solicited to attend, and hear and see for themselves, that the above Sciences are perfectly in accordance with common sense and genuine christianity.

"Truth crushed to earth shall rise again—
"The eternal years of God are hers!

"But error wounded writhes in pain,
"And dies amid her worshippers."

To commence each Evening at Half-past Seven o'clock.

Admission, Front Seats, 1s.—Back Seats, 6d.

Tickets may be obtained at MR. GIBBS's Printing Office.

Charge for Craniological Examination, 2s. 6d. Full written Analysis, 5s.

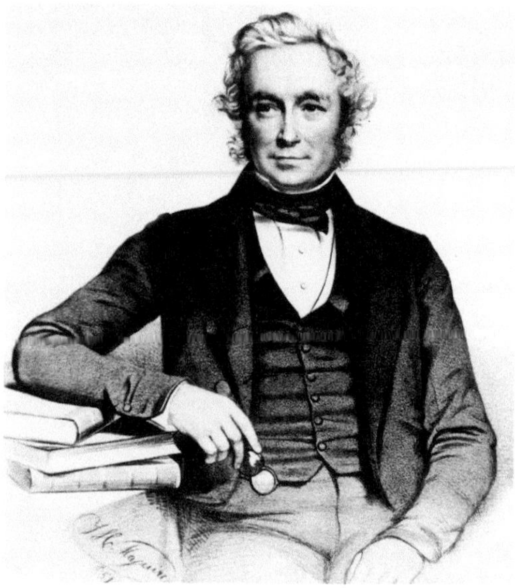

Above left: Notice for Mr Matthews' lecture on phrenology, 1849. (SAMS)

Above right: Revd Philip Stevens Henslow. Lithograph drawing by T. H. Maguire, 1851.

female beauty, respectability and worth. Also popular as a lecturer was Revd John Stevens Henslow, who spoke on botany and the diseases of wheat. A Cambridge professor, he had been mentor to the young undergraduate Charles Darwin, and when approached by Captain Robert Fitzroy seeking a naturalist to join his expedition on HMS *Beagle*, Henslow recommended Darwin, having had to decline the opportunity himself. Henslow's parents lived at Hall Place on St Peter's Street.

Music

Music was always much in evidence in the town. The first organ in the Abbey Church was installed only in 1820, but for most of the eighteenth century, parish clerk John Kent led the congregational singing with his strong and melodious voice. He was known for his complete mastery of church music, and unsurpassed knowledge of psalmody, uncommon in most parish churches. At St Peter's an organ was provided in 1725 and a paid organist employed. First was Charles Newton, a barber and peruke-maker, then Charles Domville (we have already met) and, in the middle of the nineteenth century, Henry Schroeder. Of a musical family from Windsor, where his father had served in a private band for the royal family, Schroeder was a professional, playing for St Peter's for thirty years. He composed a cantata for the 1865 musical festival in the Abbey Church, which was attended by 2,000 people. The express train from London was halted at Watford specially for those needing to change there for St Albans.

Court sessions were formally opened by two trumpeters and we can imagine that this duty was performed by the Sherman family. John Christopher Sherman kept the Trumpet alehouse on Holywell Hill in the late 1740s.

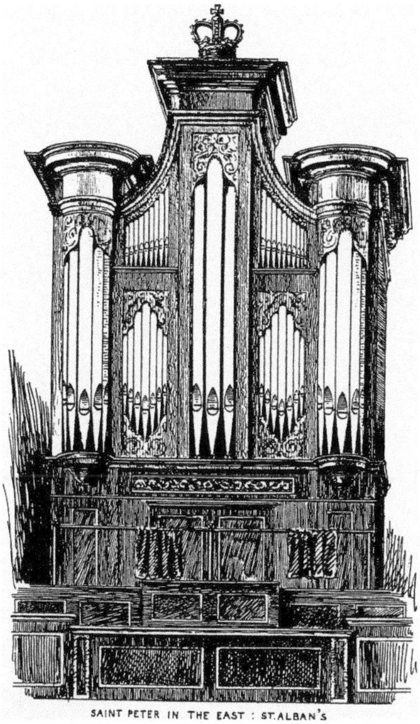

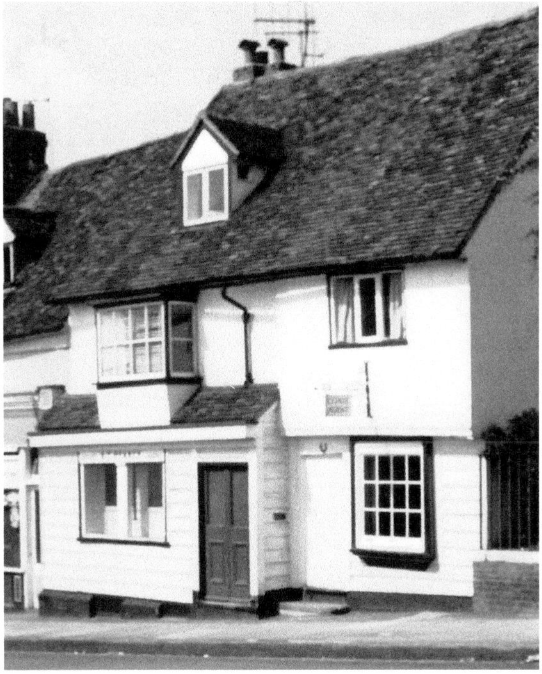

Above left: The organ installed in the west gallery at St Peter's in 1725 and removed to the chancel at the time of Grimthorpe's restorations in 1893.

Above right: The former Trumpet Tavern on Holywell Hill, photographed in 1968 by Alf Gentle. (SAMS)

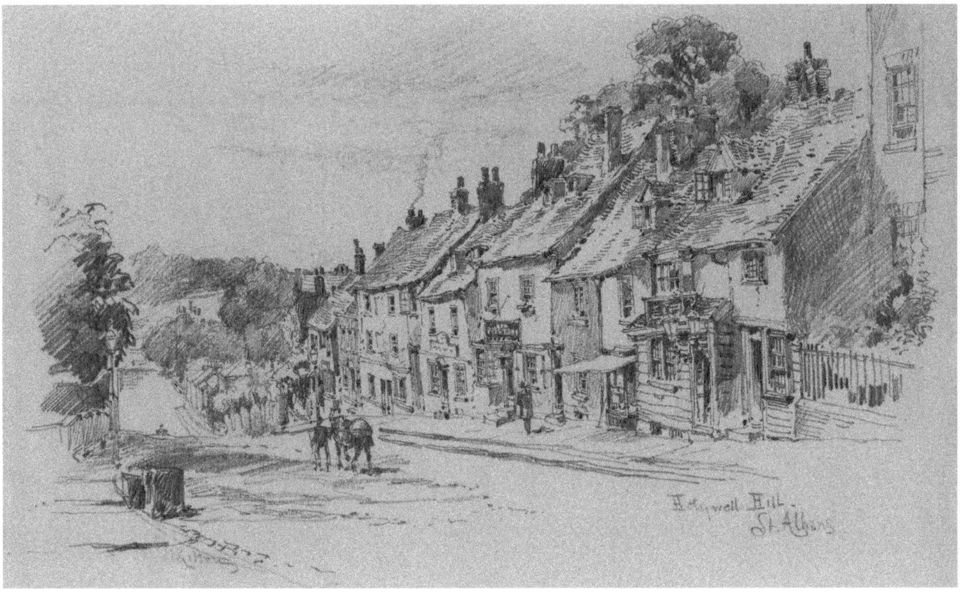

Pencil drawing of Holywell Hill in the 1890s with the Trumpet Tavern on the right, by F. G. Kitton. (SAMS)

Though then an innholder, he was later described as music master and then gentleman. His two sons were also musicians and the daughter of one of them married John Bennet Lawes of Rothamsted, where the dance music already referred to was found.

Major events were accompanied by bellringing. Ringers were paid for their work on the births, marriages, visits, etc. of royals and also each year on 5 November – a public holiday until late in the nineteenth century, which celebrated the failure of Guy Fawkes and his Roman Catholic cronies to blow up Parliament in 1605.

More Sober Intellectual Stimulus

The Nonconformist chapels in the town also played their part in the entertainment of the townspeople. The Presbyterian chapel in Dagnall Lane could seat 400 in comparative comfort, compared with the crumbling edifice, which was the Abbey Church, where, it was said, one needed an umbrella for any event in the nave.

In 1812 the Independent Church in Spicer Street was built. At these chapels one could hear the lengthy but inspiring sermons of local preachers and visiting luminaries and feel short-changed if they spoke for less than one hour. James Brown, mentioned above, a churchwarden at St Peter's, and his neighbour Charles Manners Norman, vicar there from 1824–33, were in the habit of attending services at Spicer Street until Norman's bishop intervened by declaring their presence at a Nonconformist place of worship inappropriate. Attendance at a variety of venues was in those days not uncommon, especially amongst the various dissenting groups. In 1835 Unitarian minister Revd Edwin Chapman visited the town to preach at the Dagnall Lane chapel, but took in the morning service at the Abbey Church to hear the Bishop of London's sermon in appeal for restoration of that church's organ, where he found the great and the good in social engagement, all other churches having been closed to ensure a good congregation. He then attended the evening service at the Baptist Church where he enjoyed the sermon of Revd William Upton there.[25]

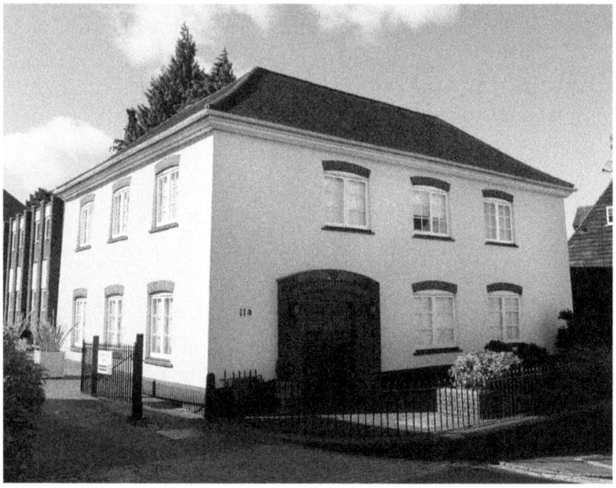

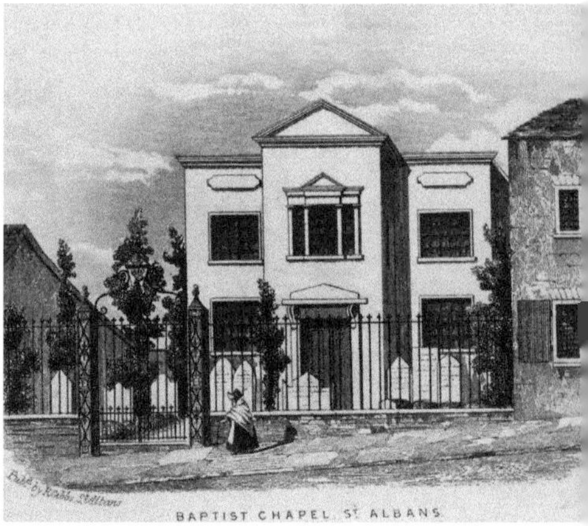

Above left: The Presbyterian chapel survives today but as offices. (Kari Lundgaard)

Above right: The Baptist chapel in Dagnall Lane where Revd William Carey Upton served as pastor from 1821 to 1865. (SAMS)

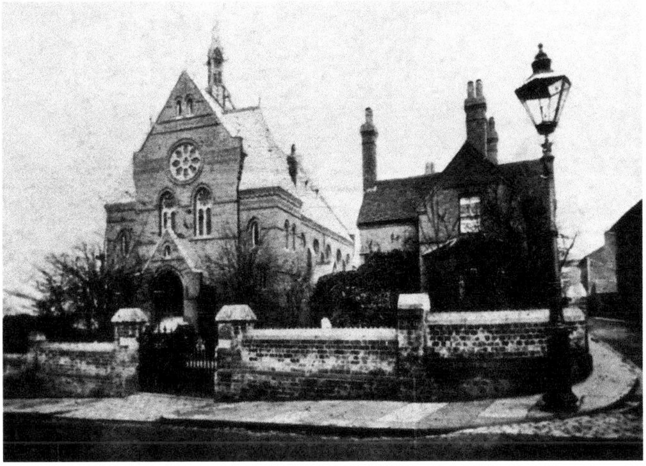

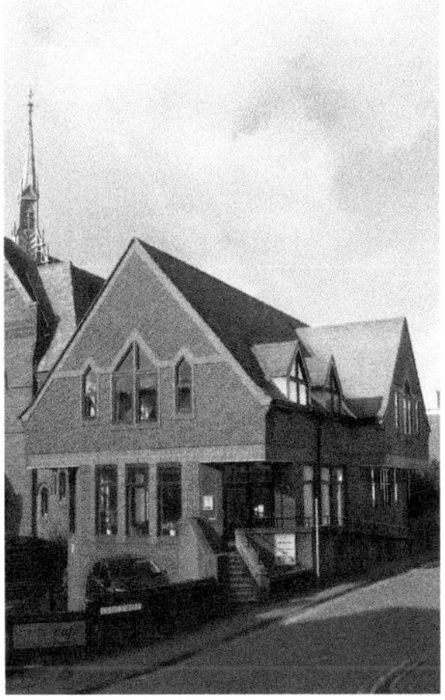

Above left: The present church which replaced the original Baptist chapel in 1885. (SAMS)

Above right: The Cross Street Centre, which has replaced the former house and offers excellent soup lunches Monday to Saturday. (Kari Lundgaard)

The evangelical work of John Wesley was not carried out exclusively indoors; an ordained Anglican priest but preaching to a wider audience than the Established Church acknowledged, in 1739, it is said, his audience in a field near the town was around 1,500.

Public Entertainment

Fair time attracted entertainment of all kinds but the early nineteenth century saw the arrival of John Richardson's portable theatre in the town. His sixpenny shows were staged, at first, on the Green before St Peter's Church. For the elite there were boxes at two shillings, or one shilling bought a seat in the pit. His 100-foot by 30-foot auditorium could accommodate 1,000 people. On one occasion, his visit coincided with the outbreak of fire at the Fleur de Lys in French Row. Richardson generously contributed £100 to the subscription fund for the relief of sufferers. Though he had done so anonymously, the Corporation, to his annoyance, discovered his identity and in acknowledgement of his generosity, granted him a licence gratis to bring his theatre to the fair each year thereafter. It was said that Richardson could stage more than a dozen burlesques and melodramas in a day. Richardson died in 1836 but his theatre lived on and there were others, including those of the Gyngell family. Daniel Gyngell's own special offering was his musical performance with wet fingers on the glass tumblers. His son Joseph described himself as a juggler and equilibrist. In 1845 he descended by a rope 150 feet long from the roof of the White Horse Inn, whilst his pyrotechnist brother George provided a grand display of fireworks in front of the town hall.

Such events continued through the century, with a 'velocipedian roundabout' the favourite 'ride' at the Michaelmas Fair in 1871, but Victorian morality was, however, by that time challenging the debauchery perceived to be brought to the town at fair time and such public spectacles were soon to be curtailed.

Notes

1. *Cathedral and City: St Albans Ancient and Modern* (London, 1977)
2. Herts Past and Present, Spring 2008 3rd Series Issue No 11. *A short journey on the St Albans Machine* by G. P. McSweeney
3. Ivy House, No. 107 St Peter's Street, the offices of Debenhams Ottaway, solicitors
4. Joshua Webster, *Practical observations on the Preservation of Health*, 5th ed. (London, 1836)
5. HALS 37963 Conveyance of the Goat Inn
6. *Uxbridge and West Drayton Gazette*, 14 March 1930
7. TNA C10/514/127 Tuttell v Mayor, etc. and other cases
8. TNA E 134 5 Geo 2 Mich 16 Deposition taken 1731
9. Stamp Duties Act 1783 (23 Geo III c. 67)
10. Hansard, 21 January 1941, Vol. 368 Col. 61
11. Trials for Adultery, or, The History of Divorces, Being Select Trials at Doctors Commons, for Adultery, Fornication, Cruelty, Impotence, &c. from the Year 1760, to the Present Time, [by] a faithful Historian, who is fully determined not to sacrifice Truth at the Shrine of Guilt and Folly. Vol, VII (London, 1780)
12. The Liberty of St Albans included most of the county west of the A1. It was merged with the county jurisdiction in the nineteenth century.
13. HALS Gaol Book II/151
14. Museum of Rural Life, Reading, FR 6/2/14
15. HALS D/ER C324/12
16. HALS SBR/290
17. Friendly Societies Act of 1793 (33 Geo III *c*. 54)
18. HALS 37969
19. British Library ADD MS 75734
20. HALS 37971
21. *Ipswich Journal*, 12 February 1743
22. Hertfordshire Archaeology and History, Vol 14 2004/5 *Town Houses Designed for Entertainment?* by G. P. McSweeney and J. T. Smith
23. HALS DE/V/F531
24. Hackney Archives M 4014
25. Hertfordshire's Past 22 Spring 1987 *Sermon Tasting in St Albans, 1835* by Alan Ruston